HEAD

SHOTS

HEAD SHOTS

PHOTOGRAPHS
AURA ROSENBERG

FICTION
GARY INDIANA
LYNNE TILLMAN

STOP OVER PRESS
Reykjavík - New York

For John

First published by Stop Over Press 1995.

Distributed Internationally by D.A.P./Distributed Art Publishers, Inc., 636 Broadway, 12th Floor, New York, New York 10012.
Tel: (212) 473 5119. Fax: (212) 673 2887.

Design Stop Over Press

Printed and bound in Hong Kong by Palace Press International.

First Printing.

ISBN 1-881616-56-8

Acknowledgments

To all the participants to which this project owes its very existence, I give my warmest thanks. It's not always so easy to be photographed. Without your generosity, open-mindedness and patience my work would have been impossible.

For their photo contributions I give special thanks to Jane Dickson, Sharon Helgason Gallagher, Nicole Hackert, Franziska Lésák, Marilyn Minter, Anita Pace, Linda Post, Catsou Roberts, Sheree Rose, Katia Santibanez, Diana Thater and Sissel Tolaas.

I am particularly grateful to Lynne Tillman and Gary Indiana for contributing their stories to this collection and for their willingness to use these photos as a starting point.

For their support and encouragement in helping to realize this project I also thank Ernest Rosenberg, Lois Plehn, Sharon Helgason Gallagher, Ira Silverberg, Klaus Biesenbach at Kunst-Werke Berlin, Christoph Tannert and Annette Sievert at Kunstlerhaus Bethanien and Art Matters, Inc.

Last but not least, thanks to my publisher, collaborator, editor and model.

Contents

John Miller

The Perverse Gesture

The point of departure is a portrait series of men. Each picture is black-and-white. Each is vertical. In most, the heads are slightly upraised, filling the frame, the eyes closed, the lips parted. The men appear to be between twenty and forty. A few are older. What's going on? Just what sort of social document does this unlikely collection present?

The exact legibility of these images, the way they might be read, is highly conditional. This latitude for dissimulation and interpretation reveals how arbitrary the expressivity of the human countenance can be; as Eisenstein once suggested, a director might fire a pistol behind an unsuspecting actor in order to produce a reaction that, properly edited, would convey extreme grief. Conversely, the simple manipulation of body parts, including the face, may produce corresponding subjective effects in oneself and others. Thus, the title "Head Shots" becomes key. But this seemingly generic label insinuates a slightly pornographic potential; one might construe these faces as an index of ejaculations happening outside the frame.

Male ecstasy, male orgasm. The man who loses control of his emotions presents an exceptional figure not only in television, movies and advertising, but also in pornography – even gay pornography. The issue is charged, not the least because, beneath the gender politics, the transaction between viewer and viewed becomes purely subjective. Stripped of its emotional identifications, the whole genre of portraiture might collapse into little more than a pointless reiteration of one of humankind's universal features. But the face remains, in its own way, anonymous. Pornography necessarily operates on the basis of such anonymity. If the camera "frames out" genitalia, odors, sounds and colors, in so doing it becomes a decisively pornographic apparatus by creating what is literally "ob-scene," i.e., outside the scenario.

"In itself," however, each portrait is rather chaste – not only because of the exact balance between what it makes explicit and what it leaves to conjecture, but also because of the tacit covenant between the photographer and her subjects on which its production is predicated. Make-believe. Usually, Rosenberg photographed the men herself. Some, however, preferred simply to send her negatives. Both the title and the steady accumulation of like images conspire to suggest, after the fact, what in most cases was never a fact to begin with. Although each picture remains a matter of some speculation, that is not the question. Rather, in all possible instances the male subject is projecting an image of himself for another. Even given the various stages of deliberate and de facto editing, the results turned out to be remarkably consistent, as if going out of control were a matter of conformity. In this respect, the difference between real and fake is trivial.

The salient aspects of the group who agreed to be photographed are easy to spot: mostly affiliated with the so–called art world and sharing a liberal resistance to certain patriarchal imperatives. Harder to discern is the rationale of those who declined to take part. Most claimed that this would somehow compromise their professional standing. (As an artist, I find the occasional request to pose before my works to be far more compromising than this ever could be.) Yet it seems that an overhaul of masculine portraiture is long overdue. One sees it burbling under the surface, for example, in David Salle's "misogynistic" depictions of women – which Kim Gordon regarded early on as self portraits. (Robert Gober later even forged a spread-eagled Salle "self-portrait" to be inserted as part of a pseudo art review in one of his newspaper stacks."ARTIST RE-INVENTS HIMSELF IN STUNNING BREATHROUGH" ran the headline – or something like that.)

One of the 1950s cliches of the artist was that this figure was a man (?) who internalized the feminine paradigm of expressivity. From this odd perspective, most of the subjects are just doing their nominal job. At any rate, the social field clearly conditions the expectation of revelation vis-a-vis what these photos actually might show. Should we be surprised when "the revelation" turns out to confirm what everyone involved already believes to be true? The set of men who could be considered approachable and the subset of those who agreed to take part both function as intrinsic, pre-selection processes.

In sociological terms, then, it is more fruitful to ask, less empirically, what, under the circumstances, would constitute a perverse gesture? Because the artist enjoins participants to expose what is ordinarily prohibited, this would seem to occlude perversity from the system of representation – at least in the exchange between photographer and subject. Again, what might constitute a perverse gesture? Simply to stare straight into the camera, eyes level, mouth closed, features relaxed, no emotions evident. These are not only the classic tropes of male portraiture, but also those of that dissident masculinity, dandyism. Andy Warhol remains dandyism's best known contemporary exponent. Although his esthetic is exclusively anti-expressive, his film "Blowjob," is the clearest precedent for this portrait series. The dandy typically fetishized the ideal of self-control to the extent that expressivity became tantamount to self-obliteration. In the mind's eye of the dandy, this fear transformed the most casual personal matters, such as grooming or deportment, into heroic struggles against the monumental forces of entropy and inertia. This price that the dandy paid for regarding himself as beautiful is only slightly higher than that demanded by authoritarian masculinity. These photos suggest that now no one need pay; it can be done for free.

Lynne Tillman

Pleasure Isn't a Pretty Picture

When she was fourteen, there was this boy, he was seventeen, he liked girls, sex, she knew it. He was passionate. She could tell just by looking at him. And she knew he meant it, and she knew it was the best thing about him. He wasn't afraid. Mostly what she knew was that he liked it. When she stood near him, she could tell. It drifted off his body, like a smell she could almost recognize.

He looked hard into her when he looked at her. She could feel his intensity, see it in his eyes, in how his eyes didn't leave hers when he looked at her. He was inviting, there was an invitation. Other boys were shyer, maybe they didn't like sex, or girls, or didn't know if they did, they were afraid and awkward, furtive about what they wanted. Those eyes would leave hers, lose hers, glance away, not look into her, not dare her, the way his did. He stared, glared, dared, he kept staring. It wasn't really arrogance. He was knowing. He knew something. She didn't know what he knew. She was eager and unsure.

Later, she could always tell who knew how to kiss, how to use his mouth, how to bite, how to hold her, by looking into his eyes and keeping the look and waiting for the glance into or away, she always knew. Her body was unruly. She was tremulous. She wanted to be lighter, fearless, and heavier, lustful, and freer, unburdened of an indeterminate weight she walked the world carrying. Her sexed body, unattended, sought attention. Attraction was received and sent ambivalently. She ached and tensed and didn't know why.

When he was sixteen, he didn't know what to do with his hands, where to put them, how hard to dig into her skin, did she like that, and he was mostly thinking about himself, his first time, and when he came, it was over and they'd done it, he'd gotten in to her, her vagina was warm, kind of wet and velvety, and she didn't bleed that much. He didn't know if he loved her. But his friends said he didn't have to. He couldn't look at his mother, he knew she knew, and he wanted her to know, but he didn't want to tell her. He didn't see the girl again because she moved away. Maybe he wouldn't have anyway.

Later, he remembered the smell of her hair and the way she moved under his body and the way she didn't move. She made a sound, a little whimper. He didn't know what that was, pain, pleasure. He never stopped worrying about how heavy he was when he was on top of a woman. He never knew exactly what he expected from sex, women, from her, now. He wanted to feel good for longer than he did. He demanded stealthily. He suffered the loneliness of his own body.

She wasn't flying. She knew where she was. His hands and arms motioned down. Their gestures fell on the ground. Ecstasy's available, he laughed. Then he wanted to touch her. He was grimacing and smiling. He pointed again. She looked down. She was adamant. Literal minded. Blood rushed in her brain and pushed crazily through her body. It made thinking and orgasms possible. He watched her. Her back was a ribbon of flesh, a river of flesh. He wasn't sure. He wanted her.

Someone else was another world.

Later, she wanted him.

She liked to lust, loved the sensation, the thrill, only when she could have what she wanted. She took a few chances. Sometimes she threw it away, let it go, risked everything, which wasn't much, she didn't care. She wasn't her body, she was. She couldn't tell about him yet, how he felt, how she felt about him.

He couldn't tell. He wouldn't tell.

Later, he entered her.

He said: You feel good.
He said: Do you think you could love me?
He said: Was that good?
He said: Did you come?
He said: I won't hurt you.
He said: Are you safe?
He said: Is this the right time?
He said: I don't go down on everyone.
He said: I don't know what's wrong with me.
He said: Are you bleeding?
He said: I think I could love you.
He said: Are you okay?
He said: Why did you do that?
He said: How do you like it?
He said: Did I hurt you?
He said: I really like you.
He said: Not now, give me some time.

He said nothing. He said a little. He said her name. He said everything he could. He couldn't talk.

She surrounded him. She took him in to her, let him in. The outsider's inside her, she thought and stopped herself. She didn't want to remind herself to forget. She looked at her body, his body. They were angling for position. They were imperfect pictures of people having sex. She bit him on the cheek.

He made love to her. She made love to him. She dangled above him. He fucked her, she fucked him, he relieved her, she frustrated him, he teased her, she tempted him. She waited. He moved. She grasped. He grabbed. She touched. He held. She clasped. He released. She contracted. He kneaded.

He closed his eyes. He opened his mouth wider. Wider and wider. He wanted to take her into him, swallow her. He looked funny to her, unfamiliar in his pleasure. He wondered what he looked like to her. He blanked the thought out, erased it. Fuck. His body jerked.

She wanted to bite him harder, even make him bleed, just a little. This won't hurt him, she thought. She didn't. She licked his shoulder, tentatively.

She was strange to him, a stranger. He was new to her but she could get used to him.

She said: You don't have to say anything.
She said: I like that.
She said: Do that again.
She said: No, not yet.
She said: Yes.
She said: I have a condom.
She said: Wait.
She said: I like you, too.
She said: It's been a while.
She said: I wish I knew you.
She said: That's all right.
She said: Are you crying?
She said: Again.
She said: Almost.
She said: You tell that to all the girls.
She said: Do what?
She said: Do it again.
She said: That doesn't hurt.
She said: That hurts.
She said: That feels good.
She said: Kiss me.
She said: Now.

In the universe of things she didn't know, sex was at the top of a long, unwritten list. Momentary, temporary, everpresent, absent, disruptive, expected, it fled scrutiny. She didn't know if she'd ever find out. What wasn't named named it.

A whisper, a moan, a stifled groan, lips parted, mouths opened and shut, like doors and windows. With sound. Without sound.

Talk to me, he said, say anything. He bore down on her. She didn't know what it meant. She was open to him. She confused him. He was alive and easier, heady. He was full. He didn't want to be empty. Later, it might make sense.

In the universe of things he didn't know, sex was a series of questions with good and bad in the answers. How good was he supposed to be, how good was it supposed to be, how bad is bad, how often is good, how long is good, how hard is good, how gentle is bad. It was always simple and immediate when he wanted it, and when he got it, it wasn't, and he wasn't, adequate or inadequate.

She looked at his face. His eyes were closed. His eyes were narrowed. His lips were clenched. Now they were curled. His hands were open, palms up. He was raw. His teeth showed. He chewed her lips, his lips. His upper lip stuck to his teeth. He muttered wordlessly. He threw his head back and forth. He rocked.

He put his hand under her thigh and flipped her over as if she were a leaf. She felt weightless, inconsequential. She wanted to be just a body. She didn't know if she could be. She didn't know what just a body was unless it was the idea, just a body.

She tickled his back. She was lazy. He placed both hands under her ass and turned her again. She let him and threw her leg over his hip and made it impossible for him to move. She was stronger than he thought she was. She held him tight. He liked that. He thought he liked that.

He looked at her face. He didn't see her pleasure. He took his in violent spasms. She snatched hers from the wings of defeat. Her pleasure was a mighty trophy.

He was freezing. She was looking away. He didn't know what she saw.

He said: Are you cold?
He said: Want something to drink?
He said: Next time we'll go to your place.
He said: I have to sleep.
He said: Want to go out?

He pulled up the blanket and covered himself. He didn't know what she wanted next. She didn't, either. He didn't know what he wanted next. She didn't know what came next. The aftermath was awkward and familiar.

She said: What time is the clock set for?
She said: I have to piss.
She said: I need a drink.
She said: I couldn't sleep now.

Naked, alone, or with him, she wasn't unencumbered, didn't feel natural or unnatural. It was weird, lying there, bare and not stripped of anything important. She felt blinded, blinkered, by her nakedness, less capable, more vulnerable and less. If she had muscles all over her body, like a bodybuilder, muscles like small, implacable breasts, she'd be impregnable.

Naked, with her, he was modest. Then he was unconcerned about his nakedness. He studied her. He liked her body, then he didn't. He wanted her to admire him. He wanted her not to care about his body. He hoped she'd take it and him for granted, almost. Embarrassed, casual, he rolled around in bed clownishly. She was harder, he thought, tougher than he liked. She wasn't perfect. He changed position. She changed in front of his eyes.

She changed position. She avoided his body. Then she stared at him, it. His penis was coiled, recoiled, returned to him. He blended into the bed sometimes. She might not really like him. He was softer than she thought he'd be. He was different from the way he seemed outside.

What happened wasn't visible.

What wasn't apprehended stayed defiant, resistant. It was obscene, how they felt and thought, and the obscene ran with the ecstatic, raced away, right out the door, right out the window, right out the frame, on a road to nowhere.

She said: I have a lot of work.
She said: Maybe tomorrow.
She said: I'll call you.
She said: I don't know.

He said: Later.
He said: When will I see you again?
He said: I'm really behind.
He said: No rush.

Being on the street was strange. It was hard to talk. They walked away from each other. The absence of sex, a fast intimacy, could become the source of a dirty joke or despair. Everyone wants to be happy.

Gary Indiana

A Night at the Taj

Room 23

He says he does not remember where he was between 10 p.m. and midnight last Thursday, that he has a gastric disorder, that there may be a computer chip lodged in his brain that produces false memories and enables him to speak French, that he does not know any Muriel, but if he does it must be a stranger who approached him at a sausage kiosk outside the main rail station in Düsseldorf two weeks ago, claiming somebody'd stolen her suitcase and for various reasons she wouldn't go into she couldn't report the theft; that woman, who gave her name as Anna, travelled with him to Cologne, where they spent one night in a two-star hotel (the sex was melancholy, perfunctory) before proceeding to Amsterdam, where she assured him that certain friends were picking her up outside the station; he then took a train to Brussels, in Brussels changed for the Paris Express, in Paris he checked into a three-star hotel in the 18th quite near a Monoprix supermarket, he's certain he stayed there at least three days before coming here. He does not know why his name came up in connection with the murder of Anna or Muriel, which apparently happened in Rotterdam, a city he's never been to, or how this inquiry made its lightning way to New Delhi. His passport's been confiscated, presumably for a routine check, and now his other arrangements are stalled. He is supposed to contact an R. Kumar in a flat near Connaught Circle, sign over some bills of lading, receive a packet of securities, fly to Agra, phone someone else from a coffee shop in Agra, exchange the packet for American currency, return to Delhi, from Delhi take a plane to Tehran and another plane to Karachi, in Karachi he's to rent a car and drive down to Peshawar, give the money to a contact there, and the rest of it he can only imagine: the cash turning into guns, the guns going over the border into Jammu, and by that time he'll be back in London, having the chip scalpeled out of his wetworks or what have you.

Using a powerful technique he learned from Sherpas, he's lowered his metabolism to a degree just shy of clinical death, the earphones feeding Mozart's *Requiem* into his head, the Deutsche Grammophone Berlin Philharmonic version, Anna Tomowa-Sintow, soprano.

Room 72

"And why couldn't it have been Victoria Frankenstein who created the monster from spare parts and set it loose among the ignorant villagers? Countess Dracula the implacable undead sucking life from the hapless Harker? We should pussify and cuntify all this dire literature, transsexualize these historical figures, replace the totemic lingam with a hole-o-rama. We need a girl Hitler, a lady Stalin, a clitorified terror as potent as the phallus, vaginated myths with all the dark charge of cannibalism and piracy."

"Bit strong for the Women's League."

"Oh? Have you taken a look at their gods?"

"Stop pacing, Bunny. You make me all nervous when you're pacing."

Room 81

She kneels with knees spread wide apart at the end of the bed, bent forward on her elbows doggie fashion, breasts dangling like bloated wine skins, glory hole and Mr. Fuzzy floating in space, while he, standing across the tulip-patterned spread, pumps his modest but impressively pointed manhood for her delectation, his skinny frame and incipient potbelly a peculiar contrast to her long, freckled Rubens of a figure. They're on their way to Karnataka to visit his relatives, mainly to dispel the popular family notion that he's queer, that he lacks his older, married brother's testosterone, that he's pissed away his twenties scribbling lame sestinas on cafe napkins while sponging off his mother and sister. She's thrilled to parade his ethnicity among her passionless leftist chums back home, while here she does a strong impression of a zesty but basically submissive near-wife, ten years his senior and therefore sensible and security-minded. This brainy big white woman spells success like a numbered Swiss account. Now he's between her legs with his fist grinding into her snatch, red hot prong pressed tight against her shin, lapping the sour sole of her foot. Her vagina fits him like a glove of slightly congealed gelatin. As he shoves his skinny brown penis inside he wonders if this time she'll let him put it in her ass. He won't feel he really owns this great white whale down to the ovaries until he sees her shit on his dick. He tells her he's fucking her fine fine pussy, he orders her to fuck that big, hard dick all the way down to his aching balls, he whispers that his balls are bursting with so much come he could populate Nigeria: his voice is a bit too piping and priggish for this sort of steamy discourse, she likes a lot of verbal but he'd like to pull out and poke it up her poop chute without a lot of chit-chat. The thought makes him come before she's even half-lubricated, he slides out with a pop and spanks her fanny with his spurting rod, his jism slimes down her ass crack as he wipes himself on her rosebud. She crawls away from him and sprawls with her shoulders against the headboard, starts doing herself with her fingers. He tells her to wait, says he can get it hard again after a cigarette. *Oh sweetie* she says *when did you ever.*

Lobby

The excessive lobby, constructed by Nehru to showcase the postcolonial miracle, acres of shiny marble that look like wet linoleum, with a raised conversation area, carpeted, full of ecru divans and plushy chairs that the honored guest sinks into and disappears altogether, criss-crossed by Japanese executives flushed from drunken exertions in a karaoke bar, a fat lady from Des Moines clutching *Asia Week* and *The Wall Street Journal* as she feeds herself sweets, a massive Sikh in an orange turban lighting a cigarette with a pounded gold lighter, and now three men in tuxedos, a sharp-faced Eurasian in his early 30s and a taller, younger Chinese man whose feral mouth's full of crooked gold teeth, supporting between them a lanky WASP, fiftyish, whose name is certainly Dickie, followed by a Danish or Dutch girl with flowy corncolored hair, in a magenta kurtah and baggy white slacks, they've just exuded from the regulation Ambassador taxi and wobbled up the steps and burst into the lobby, making it known to the doormen that Dickie's made a little too free with a bottle of Shenley's, they get this octopus of sprawling flesh over to a divan and prop him in something like a sitting position, the Eurasian says:

"Kirstin, see if they won't give you Dickie's key."

"He looks really awful."

"He'll look even worse if he pukes himself right here."

"What on earth did you give him?"

"Chan, loosen Dickie's tie. Dickie-" the Eurasian slaps him hard, smiling, "-you're home, Chan, loosen his tie a little, Dickie, listen to me, Kirstin's getting your key, Kirsten, go get the goddam key."

"Sister Mary Albert, this ere cross ayn noothing bu' plywood."

"Aye, begorrah, Father Albert, nay but plywood cood be scavenged oot a tha leprous jhuggi colony."

"Idon seem proper, bu ah suppows ill hefta do."

"This 'ere's the 'ammer Father Albert."

"Eh ken see tha' Sister Albert. Wey aright then, avert yer eyes Sister Albert."

Father Albert slips out of his cassock and stands before her all naked except for the loincloth.

"Begorrah Father Albert, yer the spittin' image o' the blessed savior."

"Thas blasphemy nearly Sister Albert, the savior's eyes was far more prettier than these here tired old sinnin' Scottish eyes."

"Sure the savior hed pretty eyes Father Albert."

"En the savior's beard much flowier en longer than this ere scraggly untoward bush of blighted Scottish fuzz."

"Sure the savior hed a bonnie beard Father Albert. En here's the nine inch nails, Father Albert."

"Well then nail me to the blinkin' festerin' plywood Sister Albert, what ye be waitin' four?"

"Will ye be wantin' me te nail yer feet as well as yer ands Father Albert?"

"I want the same's was done to the savior, Sister Albert. The crown a thorns ye'll find in the brown suitcase."

"Ah doon have a Roman spear for the side Father Albert."

"Ah jes wonna be crucified Sister Albert en fer tha' aye doon need the bleedin' spear naw do aye. Fer the love a Mike Sister Albert mind ye hit the nails not me fingers."

Room 57

"...certainly my last night on earth, which you could then explain as fear of deterioration, either mental or physical, or the cumulative frustration of an economic nightmare that follows precisely the same scenario time after time, though this is not a place where one's money worries at home figure very large in one's thoughts, it's not simply easy to see that others are infinitely worse off, it's unavoidable, there is *no empty space*, no existential vista likely to remind you that you are alone in the world, quite clearly you aren't, but this is what being alone in the world will be for everybody in the future, a dense cluster of miseries with unbelievable variations spread like marmite over every square inch of public space, and little oases belonging to the rich walled off with sentry boxes and armed guards at every entrance, it's a plain fact that this country with "the largest middle class in the world" yearns for a cleansing epidemic that would kill off three or four hundred million to clear some breathing space for the survivors. Even if you do not regard the human being as the worst disaster thrown up by evolution, it's impossible to view the fetus worship of the various religionists as anything other than a virulent psychosis, confronted as you are, every day, with the spectacle of thousands whose lives, all hypocrisy aside, are completely worthless. I mean worthless in the sense of having *no chance* of development, and *no value* in the eyes of the society they inhabit. You quickly forget all the liberal pieties and improving schemes suggested by the sight of a single homeless beggar when you multiply the beggar by a hundred million and add the concept of bad karma...

"To return to my own case, which in light of the above strikes me as extremely trivial, I wish my real intentions could be interpreted in the untragic way that I myself see them. Let's say that a failure of will that I almost surely could have overcome had I been a slightly different person, plus several small but alarming changes in my physiology, have persuaded me that it is not *necessary* to go on. Suicide is not a repudiation of life but a refusal of specific conditions in which a particular life is lived: to substitute some set of abstract principles for the concrete facts I can lay out in front of me strikes me as an excessive evil, since this is the modus vivendi of Catholicism, Buddhism, Hinduism, Islam, and all the other fraudulent, poisonous systems of control our unfortunate species has concocted to oppress and ruin itself..."

Majestic Rooftop Gardens

"He's out. What's that?"

"Garlic chicken. Want some?

"He looks really bad, Alain."

"What's he got"

"Well, there's a camera. Passport, I think a folder of traveller's checks, he must have put a lot of his things in the safe."

"That's no problem. He got in yesterday around 3, so the night staff doesn't know what he looks like."

"I think he's dead, actually."

"That isn't likely."

"He's not breathing."

"Don't give it another thought. You and Chan go back to the Sheraton. Leave me the key, I'll come round in a half an hour. Here, try this chicken. It's scrumptious."

...Such questions were repeatedly asked to the girl who had been allegedly raped for about four months by eight persons, including five policemen, two years ago...Hamida (not her real name) can speak only Bengali.

"David, I want to go home."

Her interpreter Roma Debadrata, reader, Modern Indian Languages, Miranda House, Delhi University, was interrupted many a time by the family members and relatives of the accused.

"Don't be silly, Moira. We've practically only just got here."

The court proceedings were disrupted for about 10 minutes when a woman charged Mrs. Debadrata of doing wrong interpretation. "Yeh aurat galat bol rahi hai" *(This woman is telling lies).* "Hamida ne Mehtab ka naam nahi liya" *(Hamida did not name Mehtab)...*

"I can't bear it, David. The noise. The people. They're speaking English but you can't understand a word they say."

"Rashid used to do galat kaam *(wrong things) with me during the night in his jhuggi cluster," she said. Asked what does she mean by* "galat kaam", *Hamid said* "izat lutna" *(rape).*

"And the way they look at us. Everyone staring all the time."

...On 10 August, between 300 and 350 gm of weapons-grade Plutonium-239, professionally packaged, was discovered in the luggage of two Spaniards and a Colombian arriving in Munich from Moscow aboard a Lufthansa airliner.

"We're white, Moira, to them we look like gods. Dreadful but there it is. At least they don't want to kill us the way they would in some

Muslim country. You've been under so much stress darling. If we go back now we'll have to deal with reporters and lawsuits and everything that was driving us both mad."

It takes, of course, much more to build a bomb: 22 pounds of highly-enriched Plutonium-239 or 26 pounds of highly-enriched Uranium-235. But the point about the smuggling is that it enables an illegal bomb-assembler like Pakistan to receive small amounts over time.

...Among the cuts suggested by the CBFC is the famous nude scene, in which Phoolan Devi is stripped naked and dragged across the village square and a reduction in the duration of two of the many rape scenes in the film.

"But this awful religion of theirs. Leaving the dead out for vultures."

"That isn't Hinduism, Moira, it's the Zoroastrians, and they're dying out. Hardly any left."

"Even so. Those vicious monkeys we saw this afternoon. Hateful, evil things. It's things like...that man today. Crawling through traffic on all fours. I can't bear it, I really can't. Don't look at me like that."

The CBFC also said that the claim at the beginning of the movie that it was a "real story" of Phoolan Devi's life should be replaced with "based on research."

...The nine LTTE men who vanished had been arrested under the Terrorist and Disruptive Activities (Prevention) Act (TADA). Six of them were part of the crew of the LTTE vessel Tongnova, which was intercepted by Navy and Coast Guard vessels of the Karaikal

coast in Tamil Nadu on November 8, 1991.

"But darling the chap had a broken spine, what did you expect him to do?"

The vessel was ferrying ingredients for making explosives, wireless transmitter sets, empty jerry cans, and so on...the "Q" branch of the Tamil Nadu police...is "convinced" that they scaled the 24-foot (7.2 - metre) wall, using bed-sheets as ropes.

"But those stumps, David, the man had leprosy as well."

The nine had walked out around 10:30 p.m. out of two adjoining cells, whose locks were missing, revealing the complicity of the jail officials.

"You can't catch leprosy from looking at someone, whatever put that idea in your head?"

Corridor

Something is not right. He fears the telling, overlooked detail, closing the door with the Do Not Disturb face outward, down in the elevator to reception, waving the key, he says he's Richard Johnson from Detroit, America, the desk clerk eyes him with a wary look and asks for his passport, fortunately he's used his little kit to lift out Dickie's photograph and glue in his own. The metal box is a disappointment, one Rolex watch and about eight hundred in U.S., an air ticket he probably can't peddle and certainly can't use, then back to the ninth floor, in the room he regrets that he's only filled a small shampoo bottle with gasoline, he starts gathering flammables into a rough mound extending from the balcony to the door, at least this will create a wall of fire, the trick is getting it to spread to the other rooms, causing as much confusion as possible. The towels can act as a fuse, giving him time to slip out of the hotel before all hell breaks loose. Another thought occurs to him. He could, perhaps, pitch Dickie's body over the balcony after setting the drapes going, and simply climb over the ledge to the balcony next door, and then it would look as if Dickie jumped in panic. He changes his mind again. The other way they'll suppose he fell asleep with a lighted cigarette. Maybe not. What to do? He lies down beside the corpse on the bed, pondering the best technique. He finds the inert lump of Dickie irritating, he wants to shake him and say, You're no help, are you. Gone to your great reward after fifty years of meaninglessness. Dickie doesn't have to think about burning down the hotel or anything else. Alain always ends by envying people he's done away with, for exactly this reason, that they no longer have to think of anything, having passed over to a state of perfected indifference, whereas he– and now he pours himself a glass of water from the pitcher and swallows a few of his yellow energizers –can never stop calculating, never come to rest, and it's usually now, after tabulating his resentments and adding up the take, that the bad feelings come, and the urge to fuck death in the ass overwhelms him. As he tugs Dickie's belt loose and yanks Dickie's trousers down he hates this big dead Yank and the cosmic secret that's crawled up and disappeared inside him, and hates himself for what he is about to do.

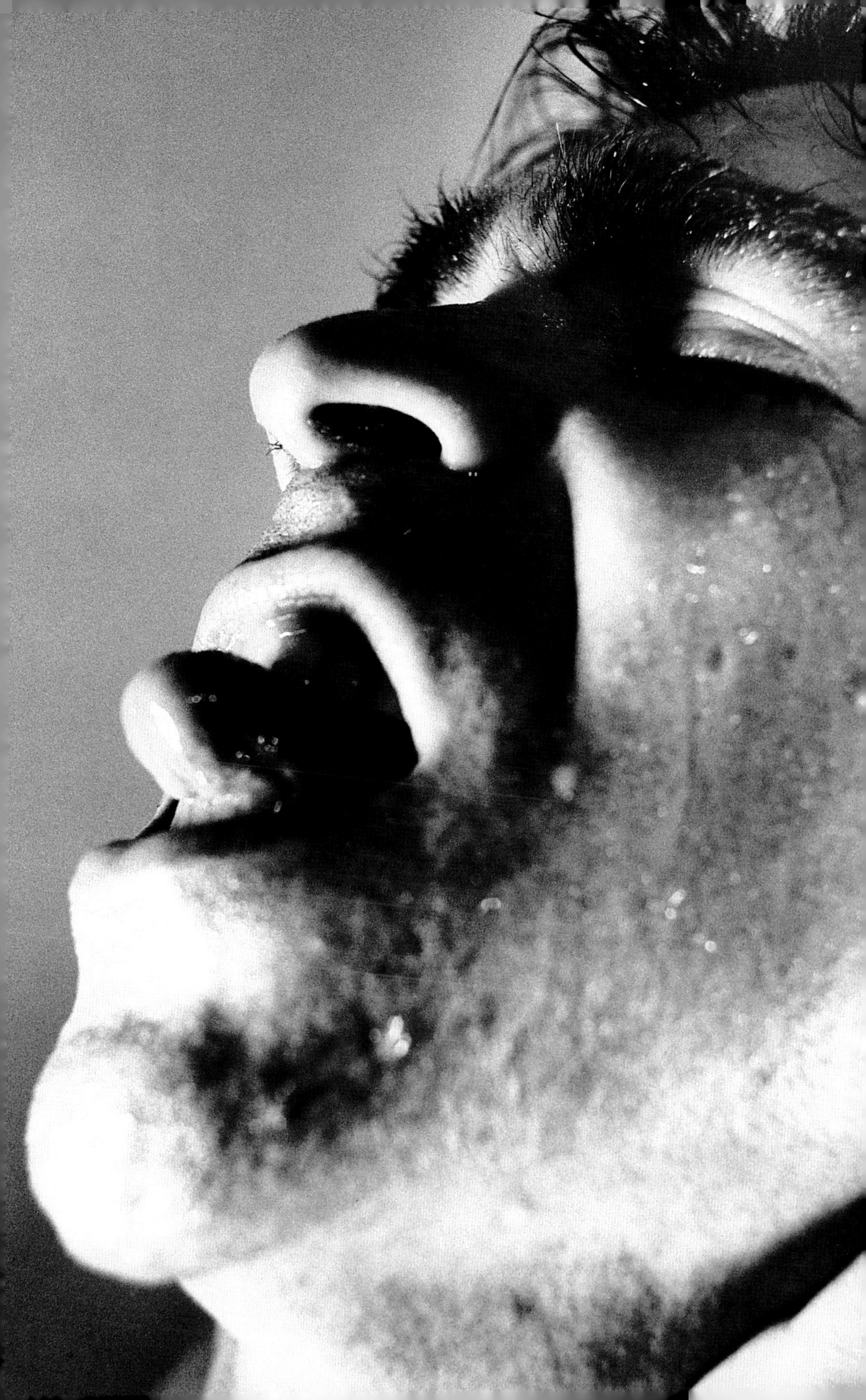

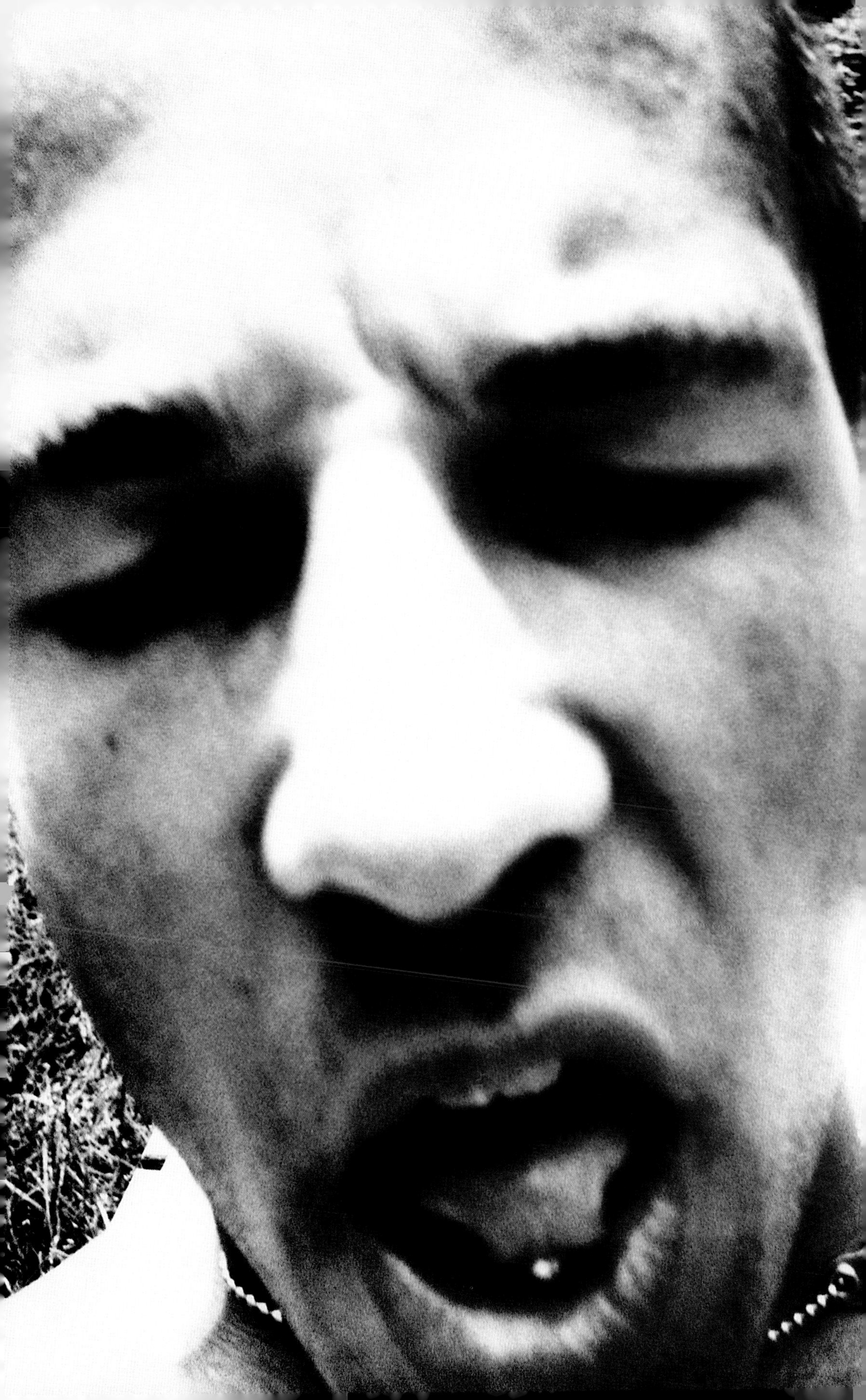

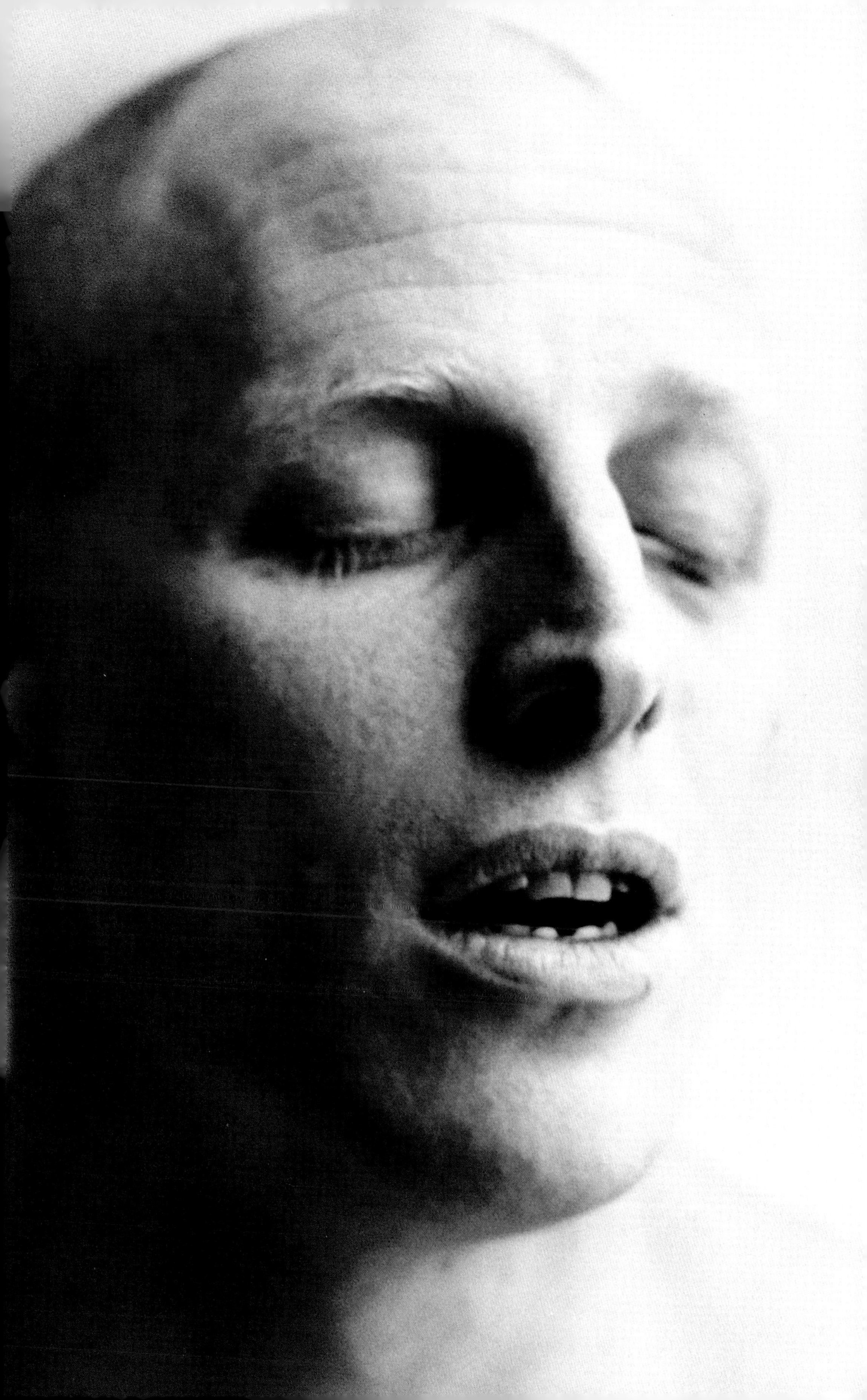

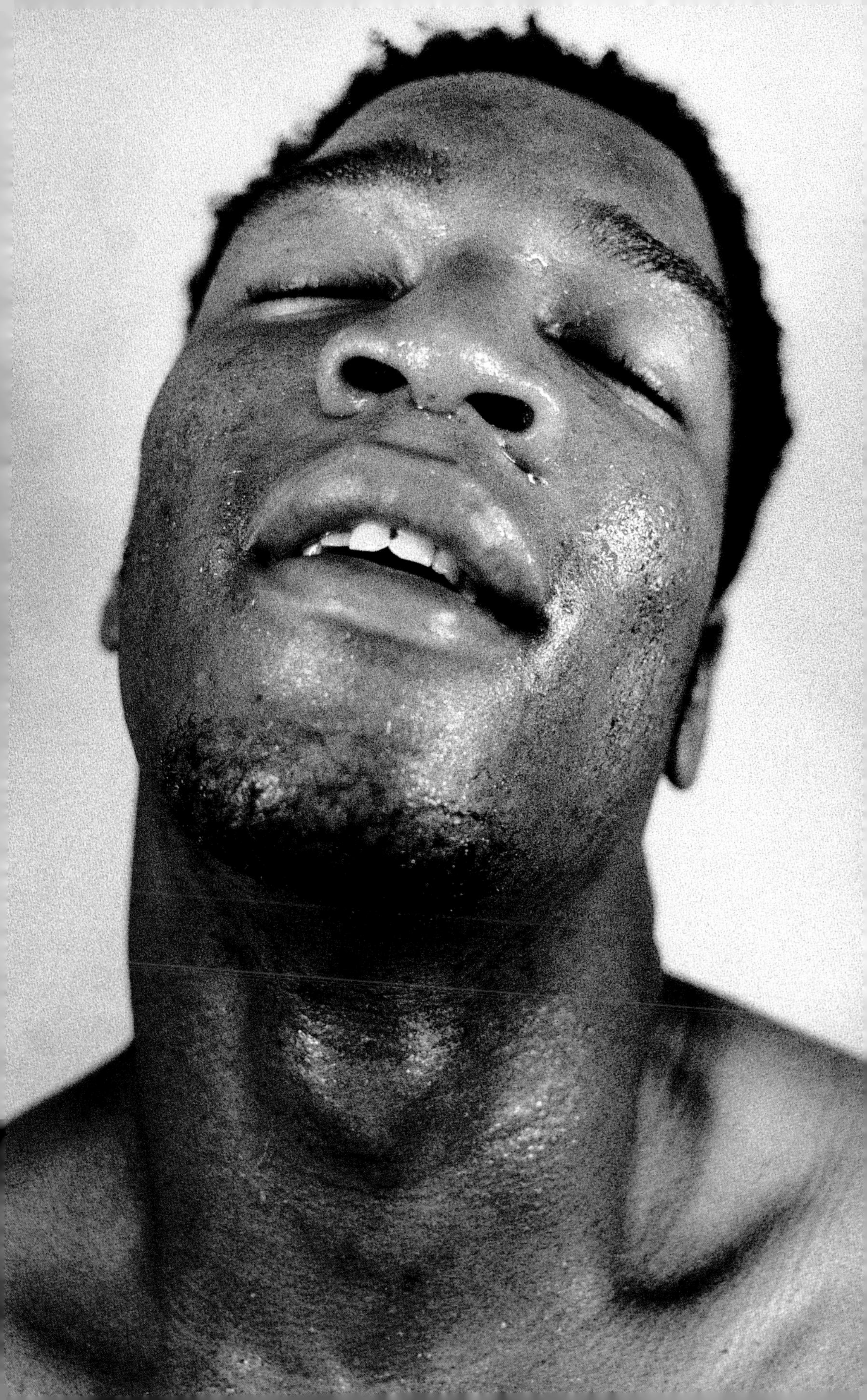

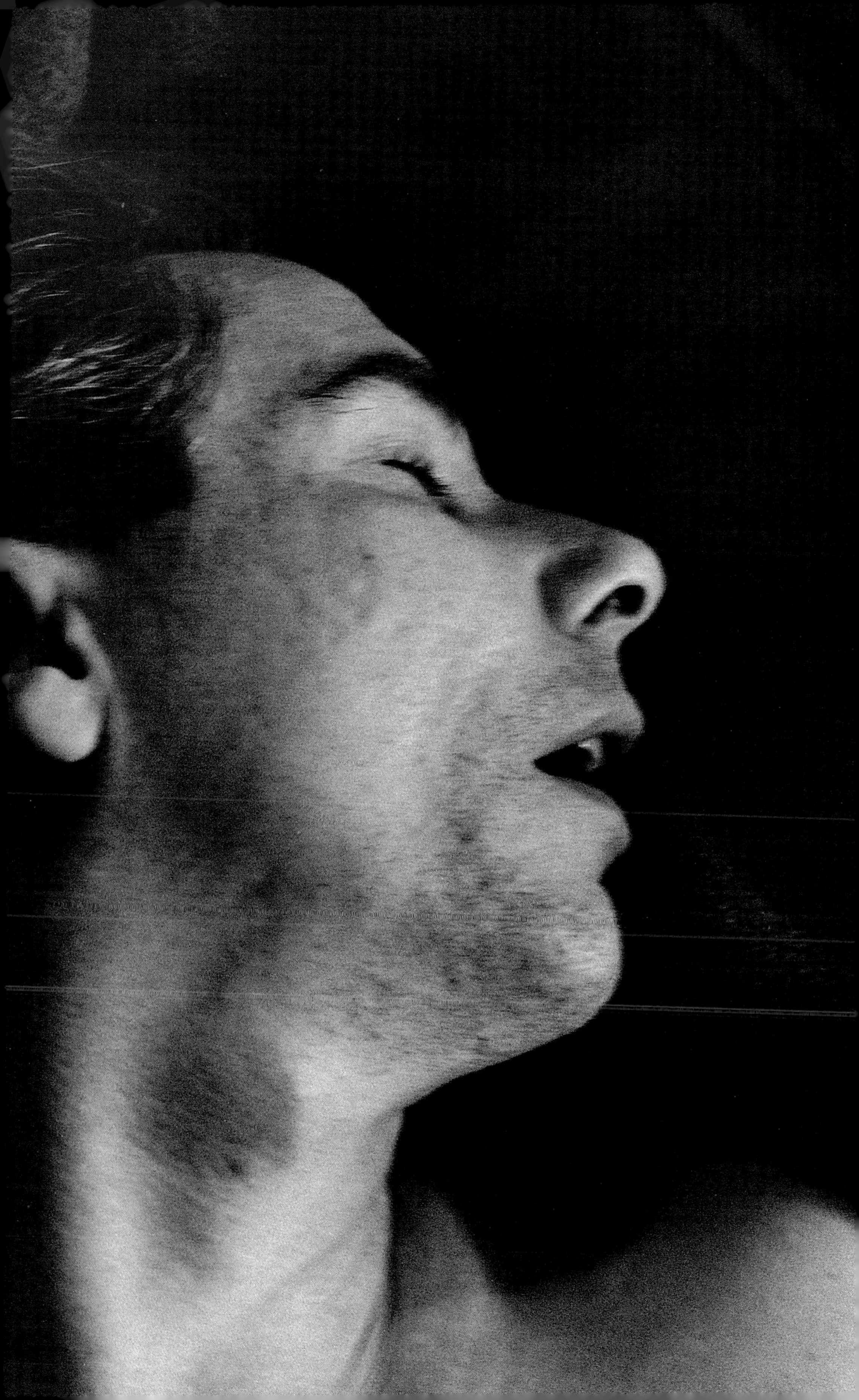

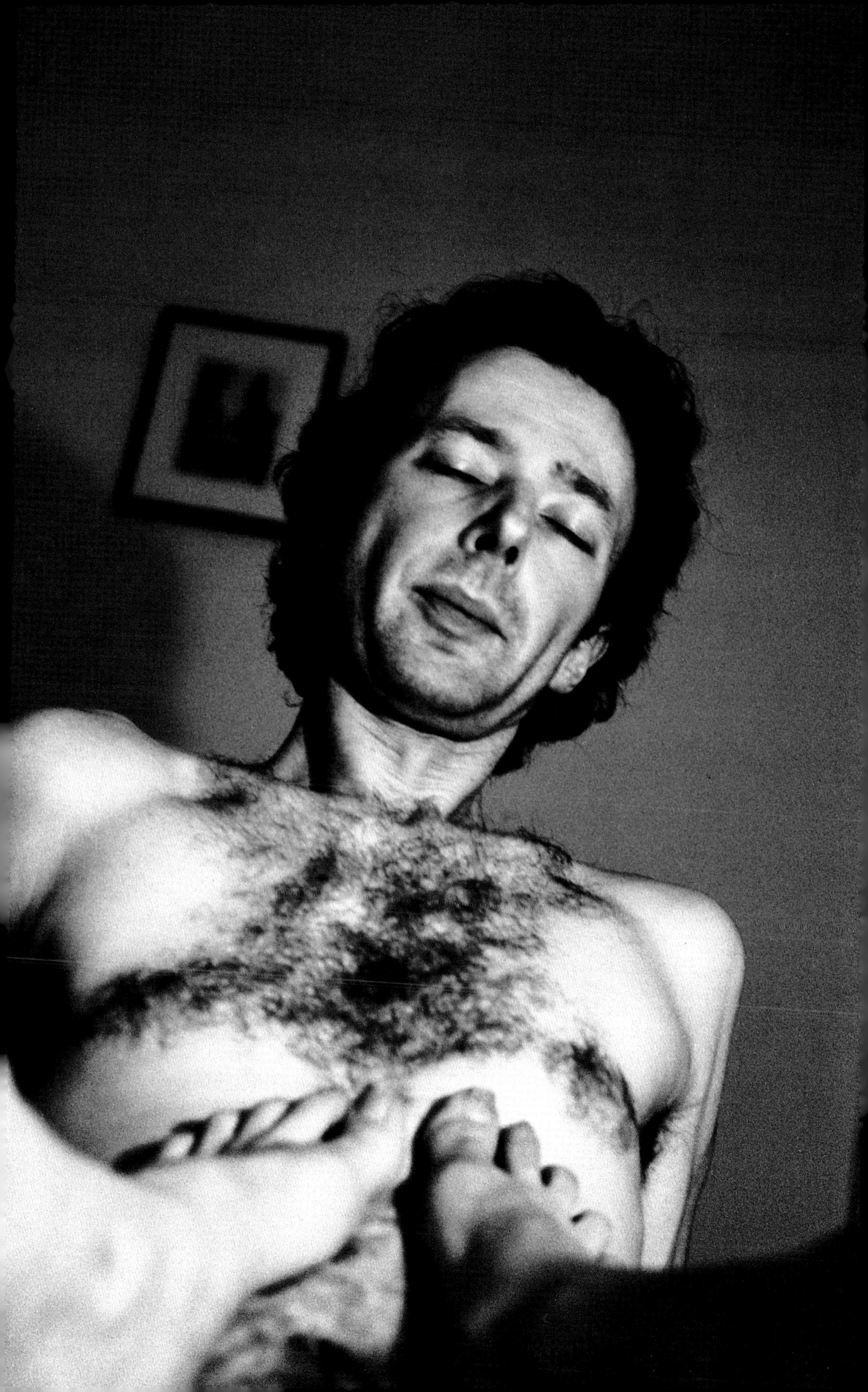

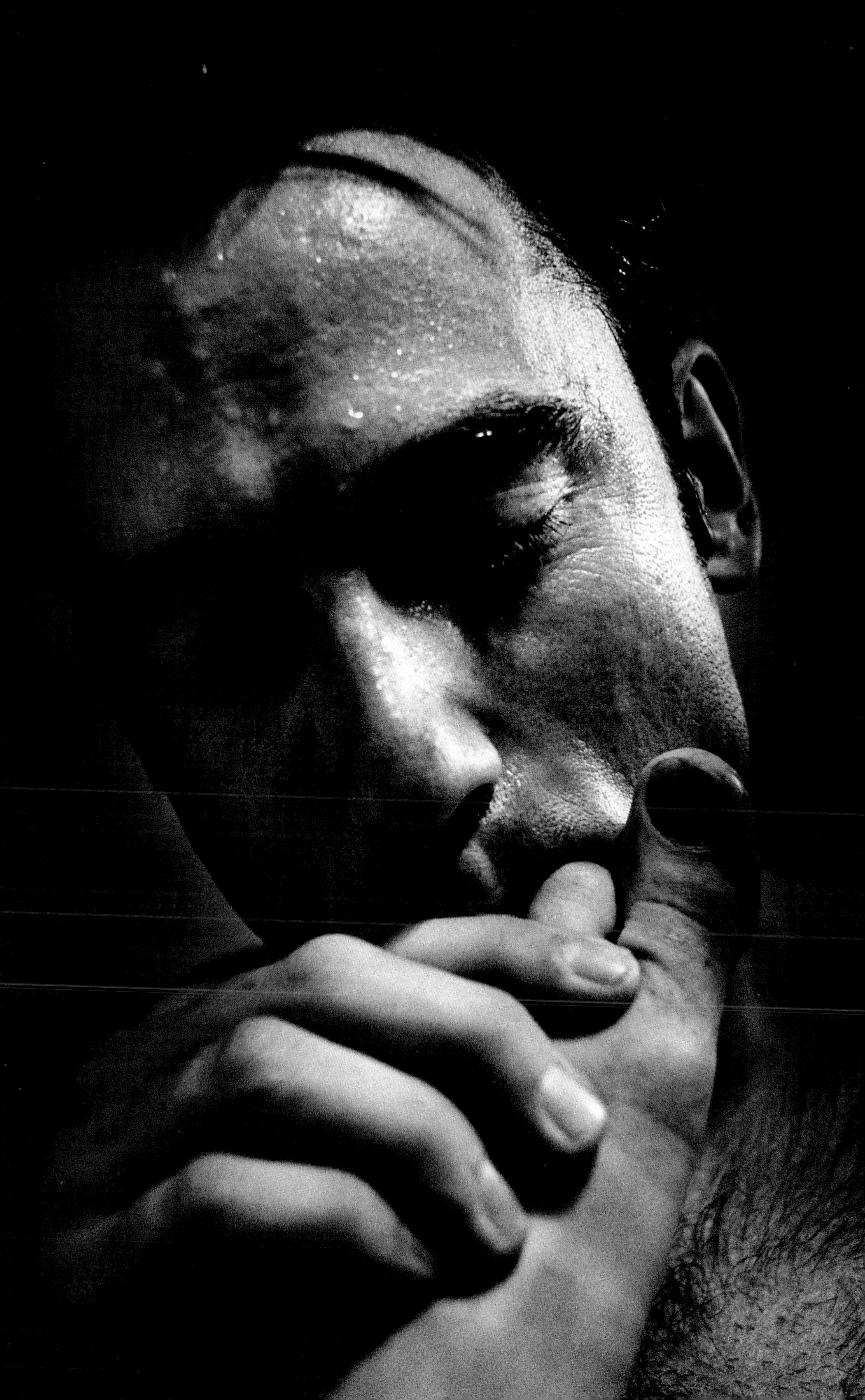

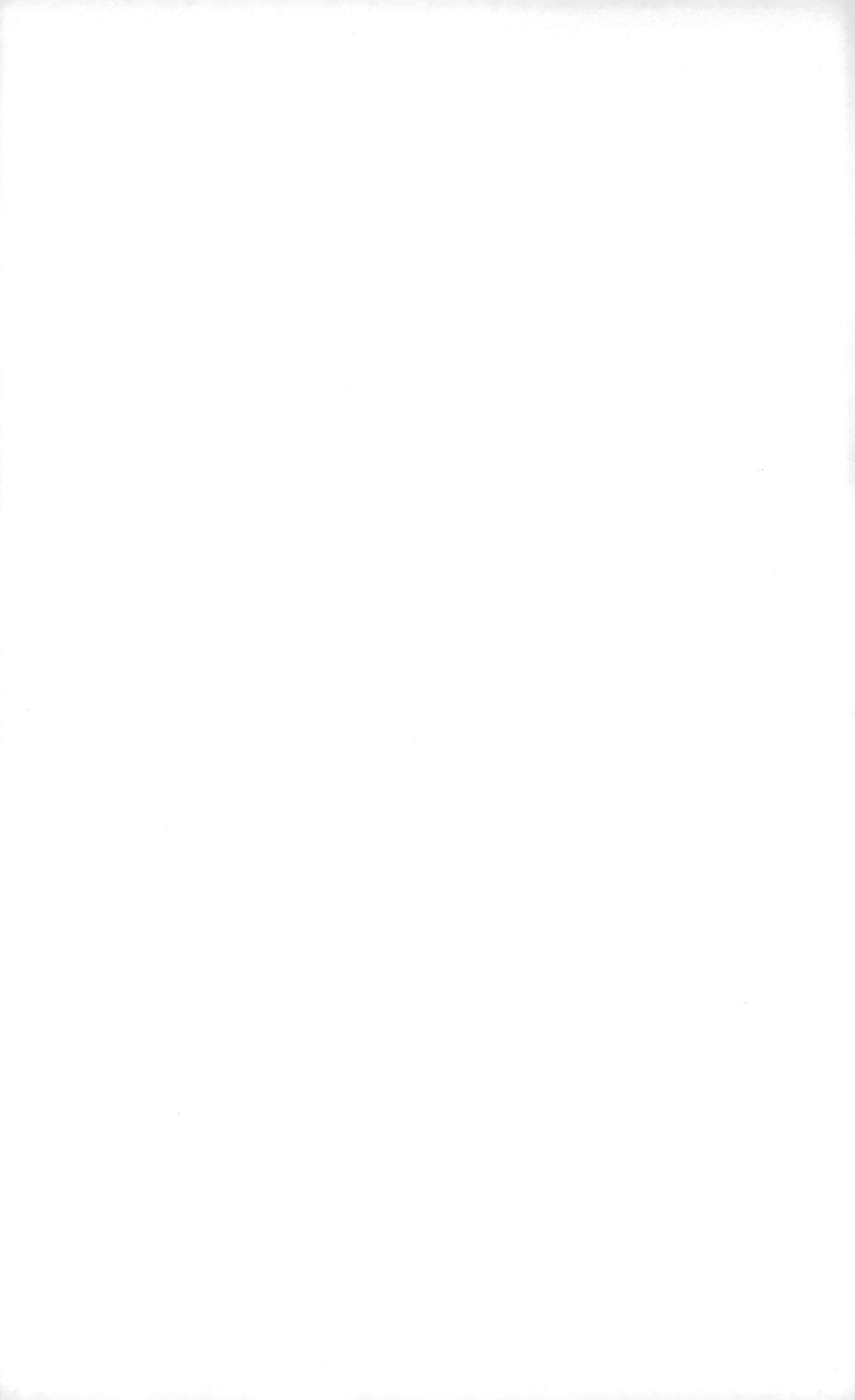

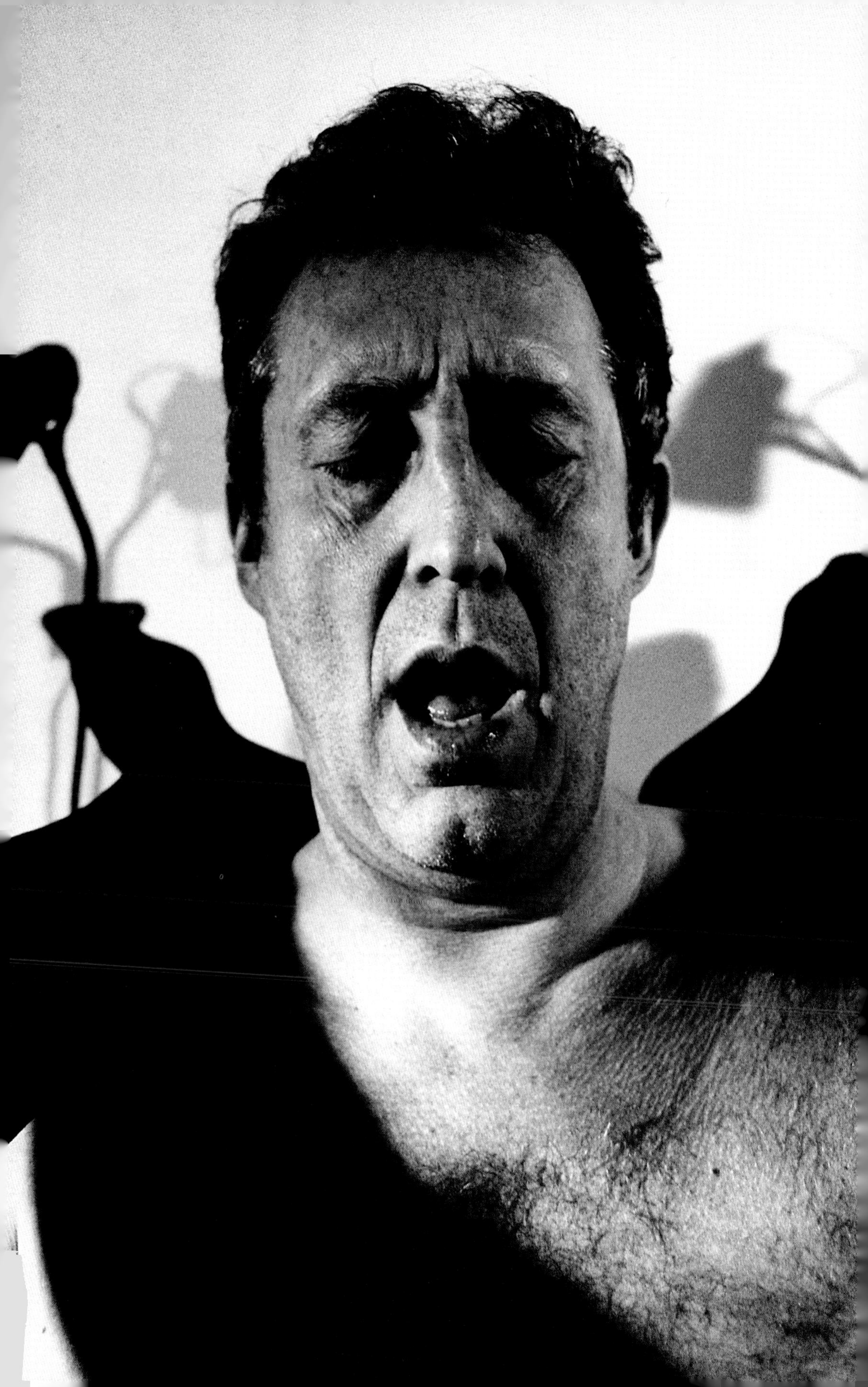

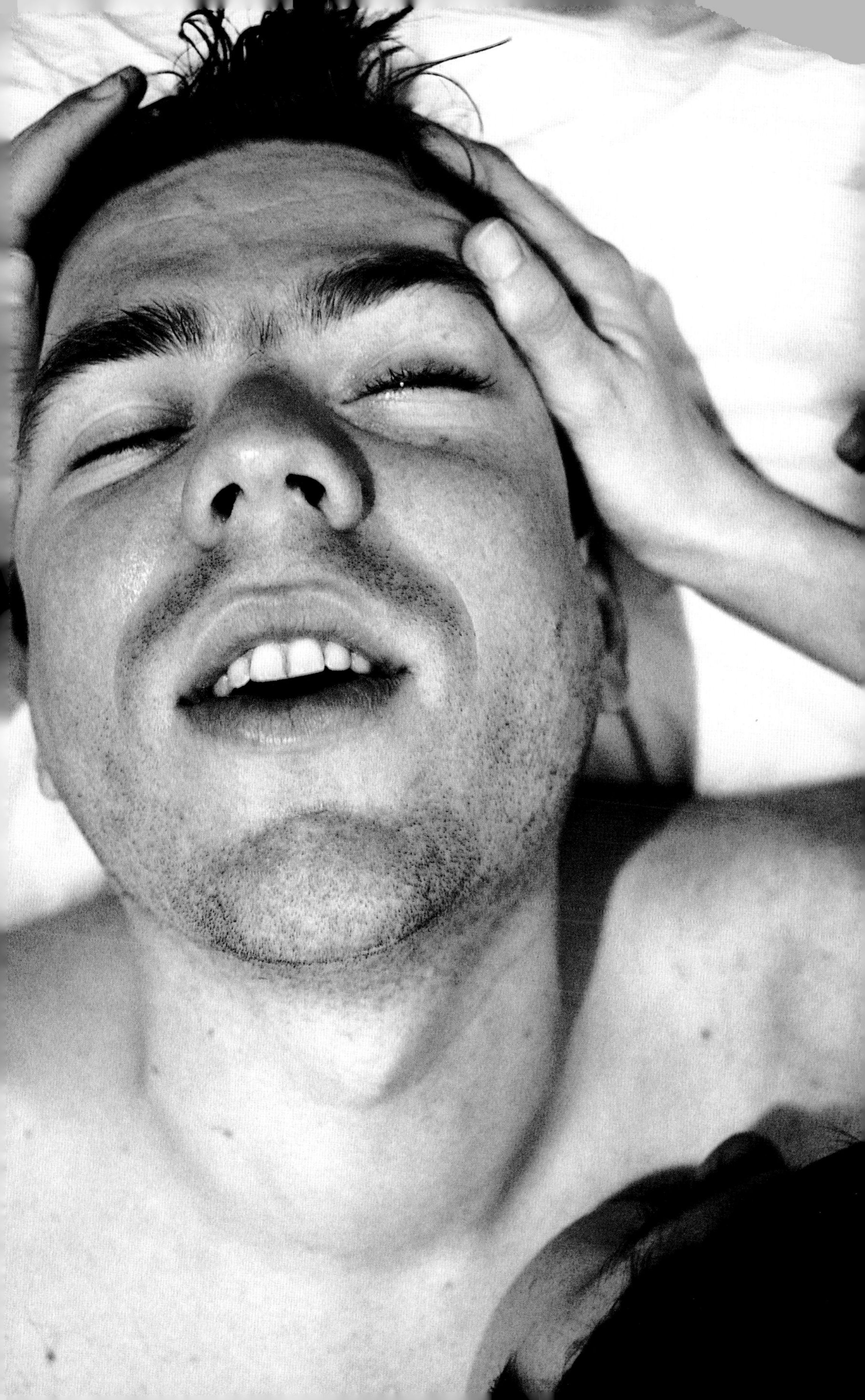

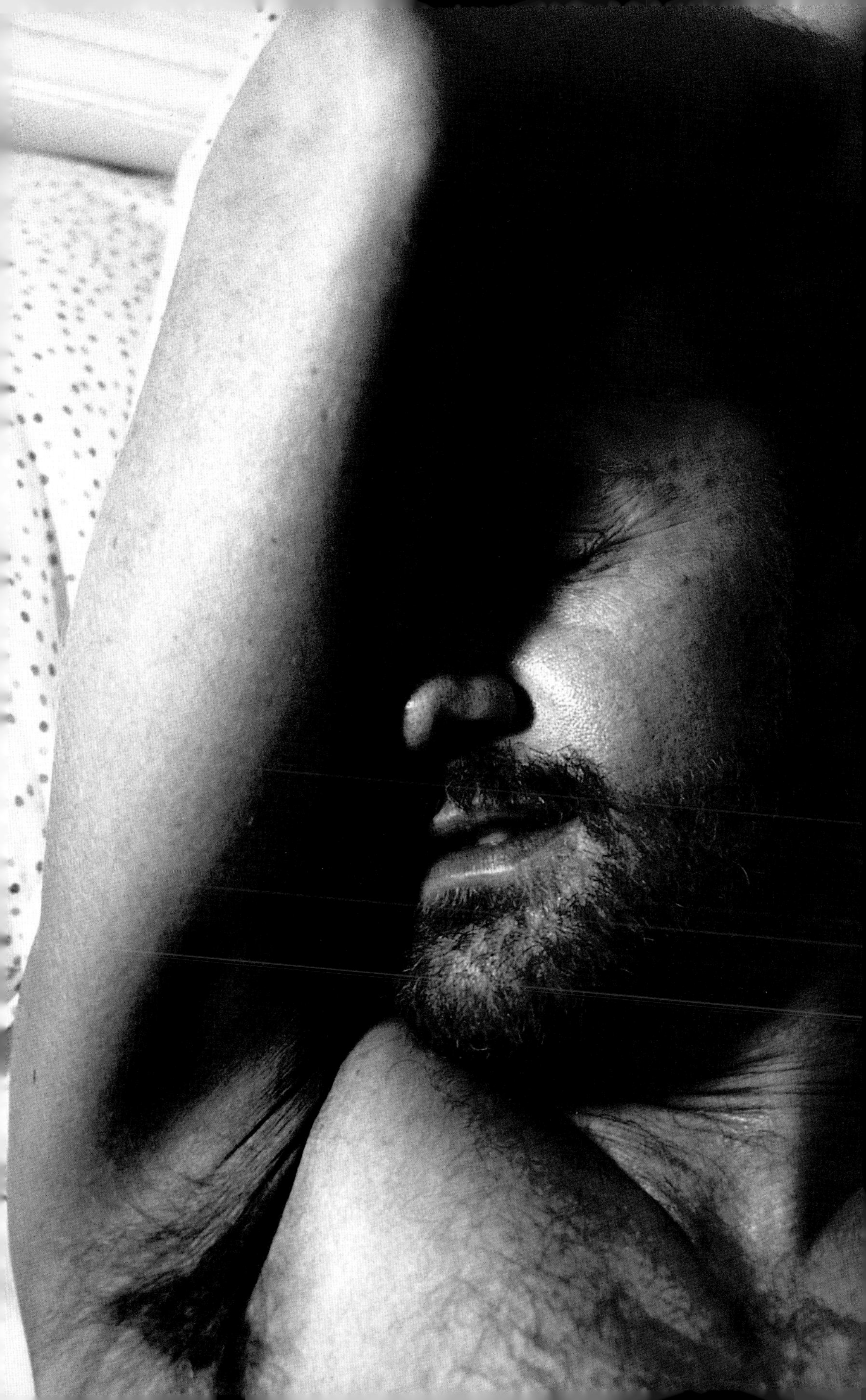

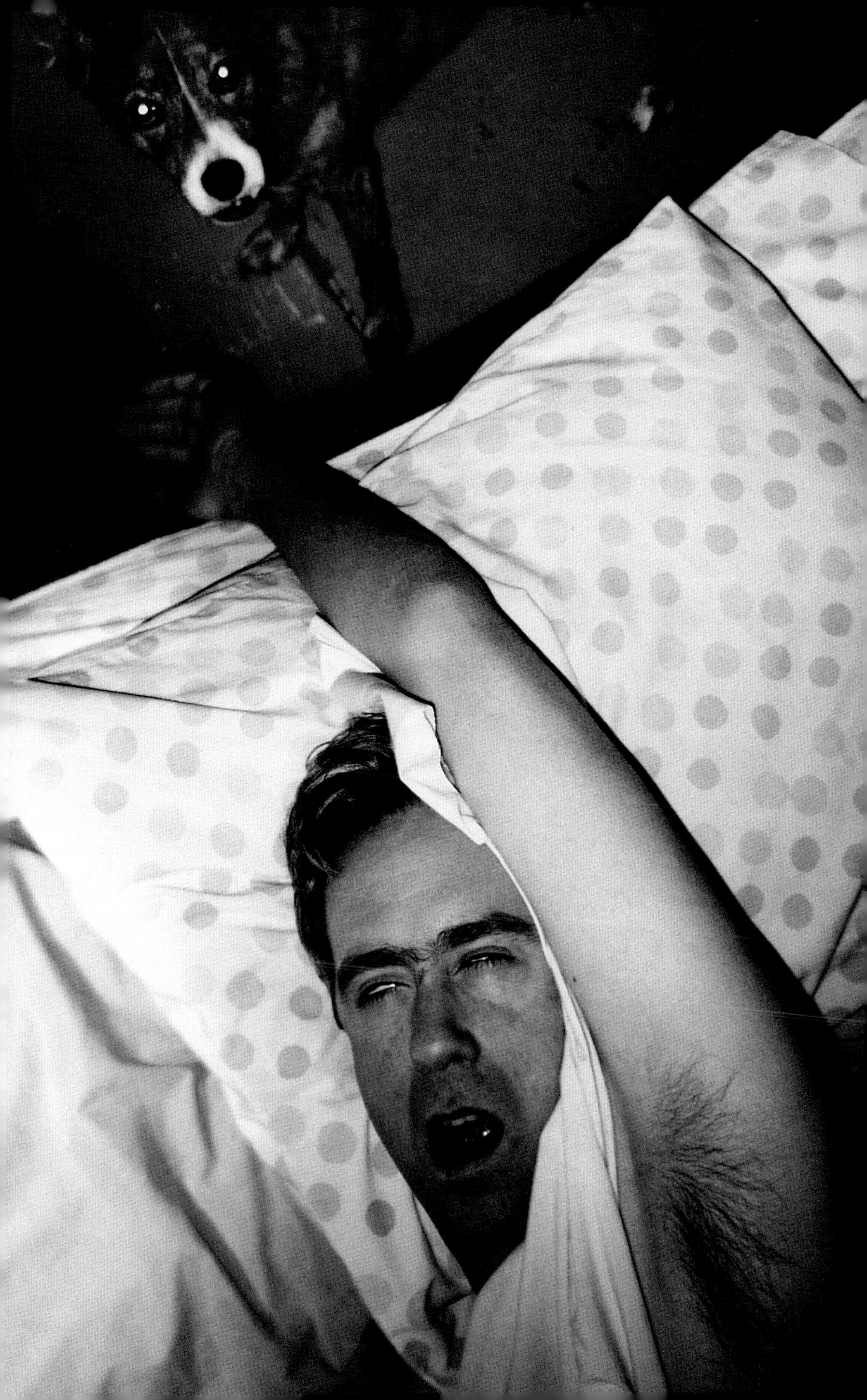

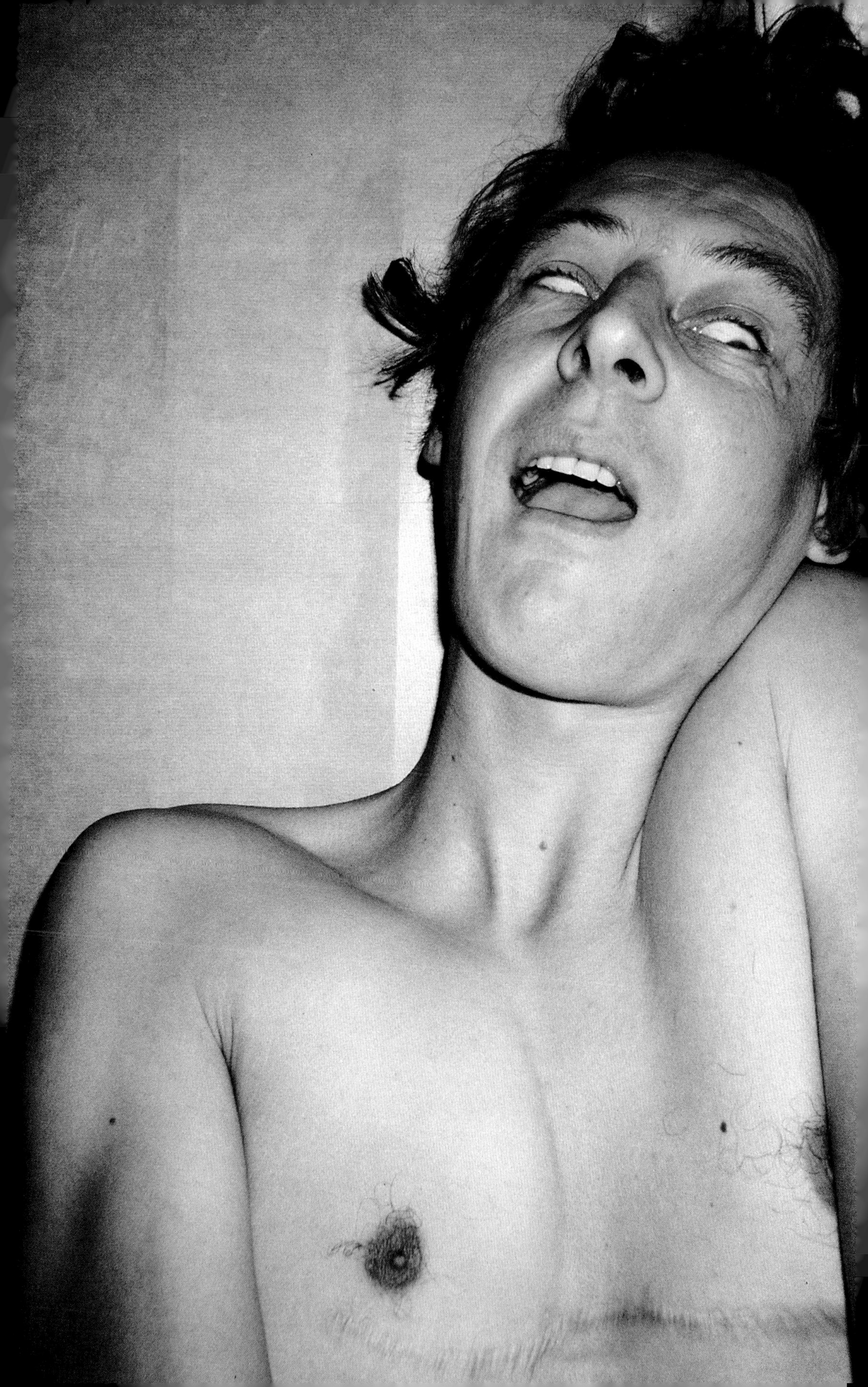

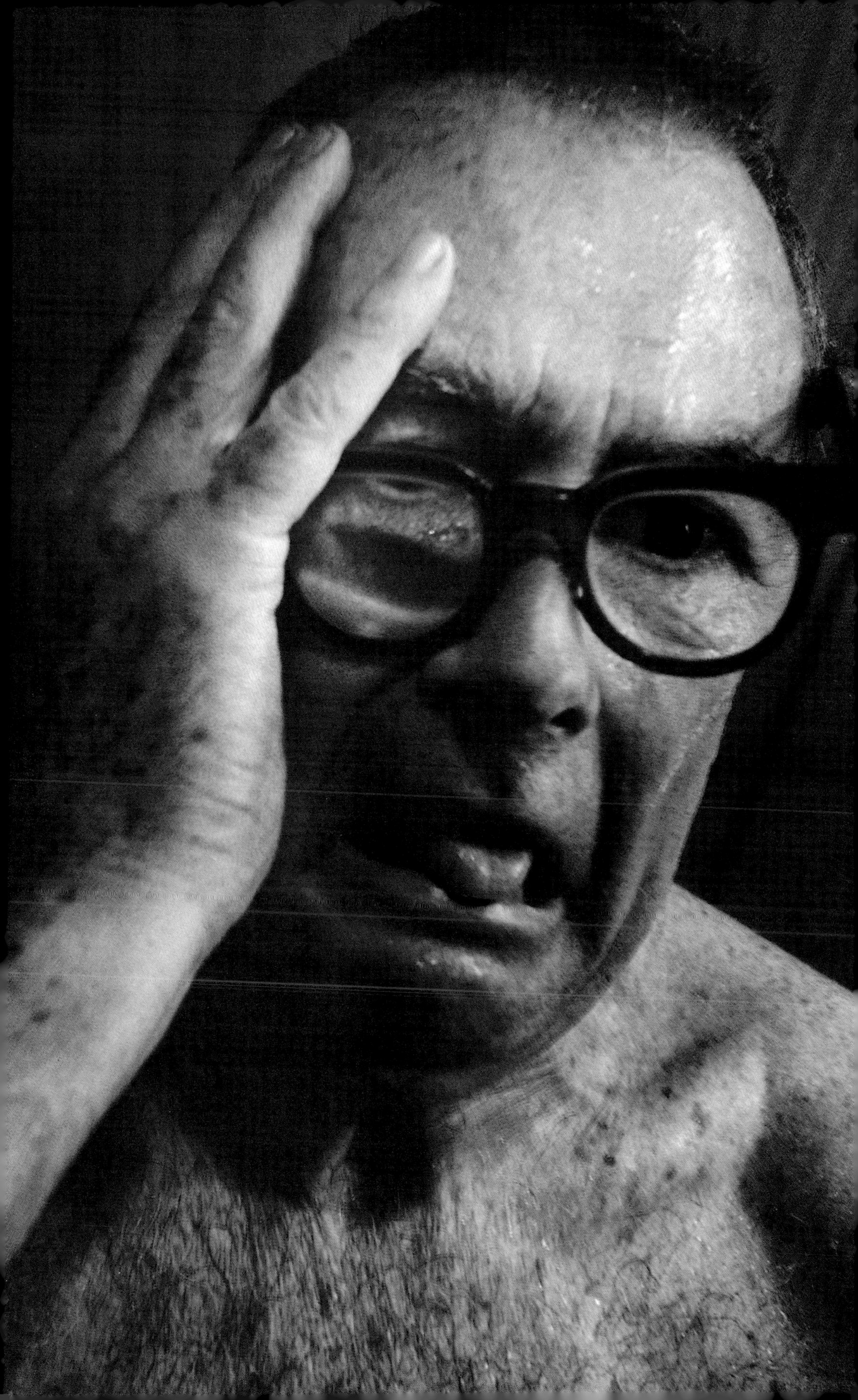

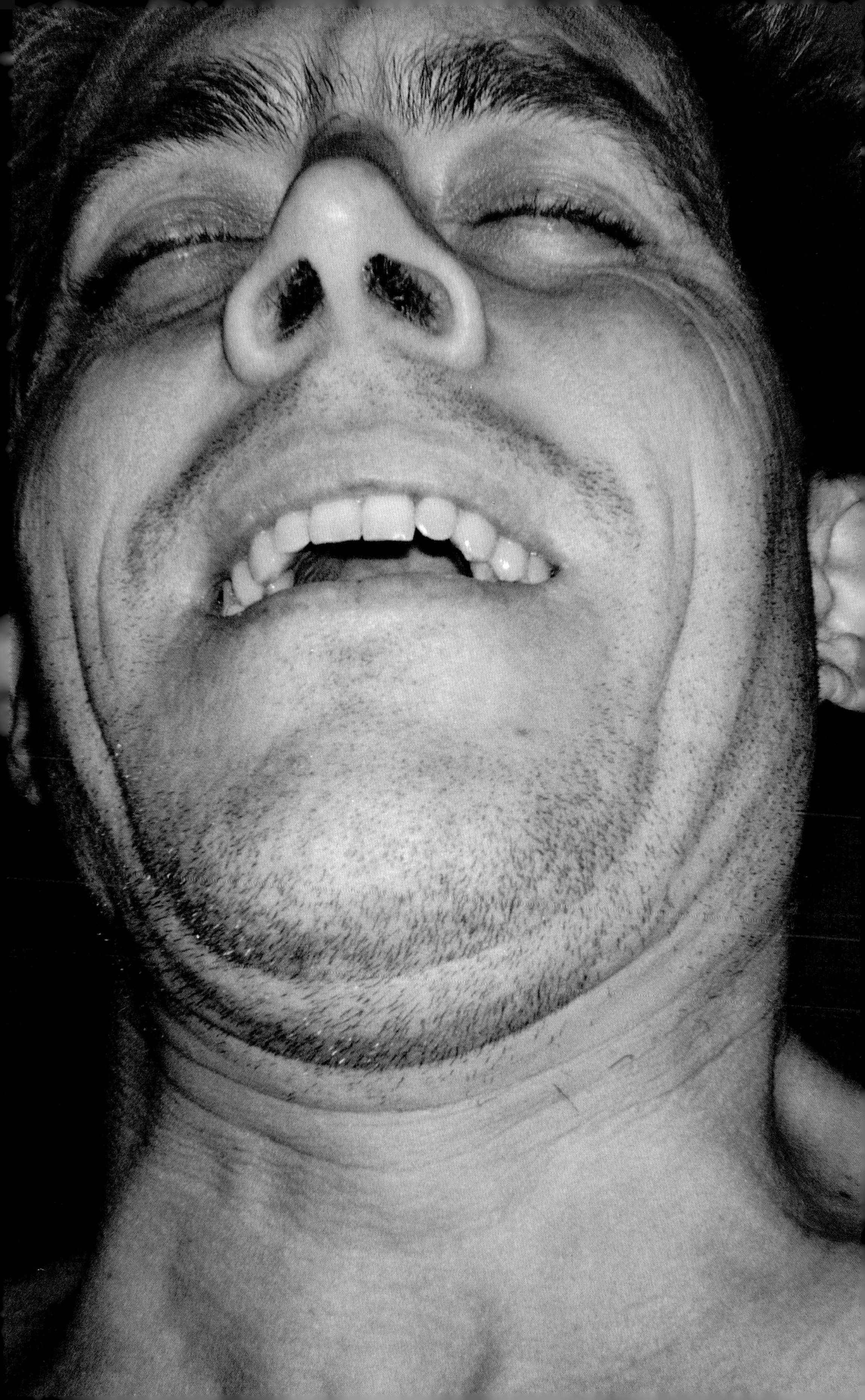

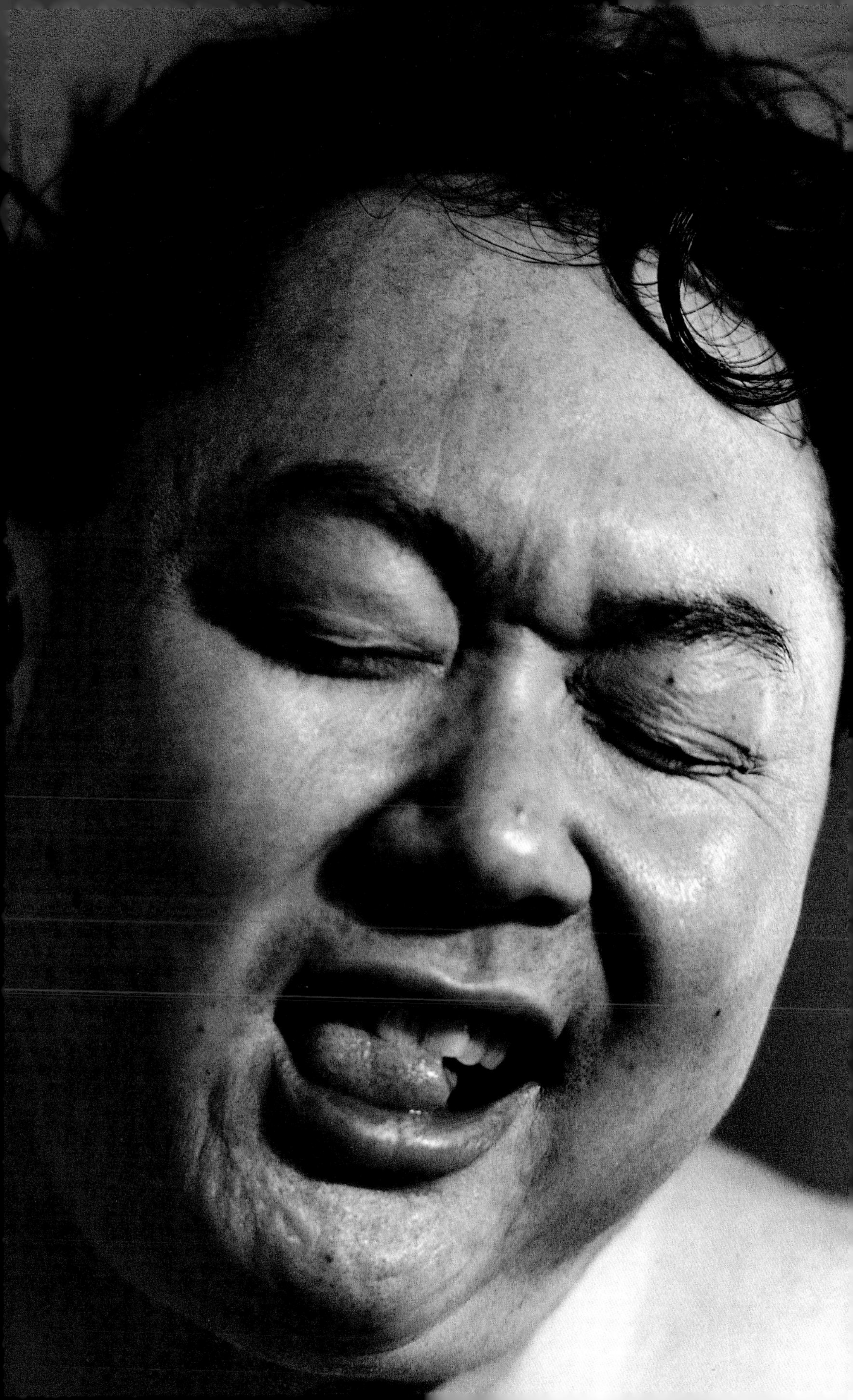

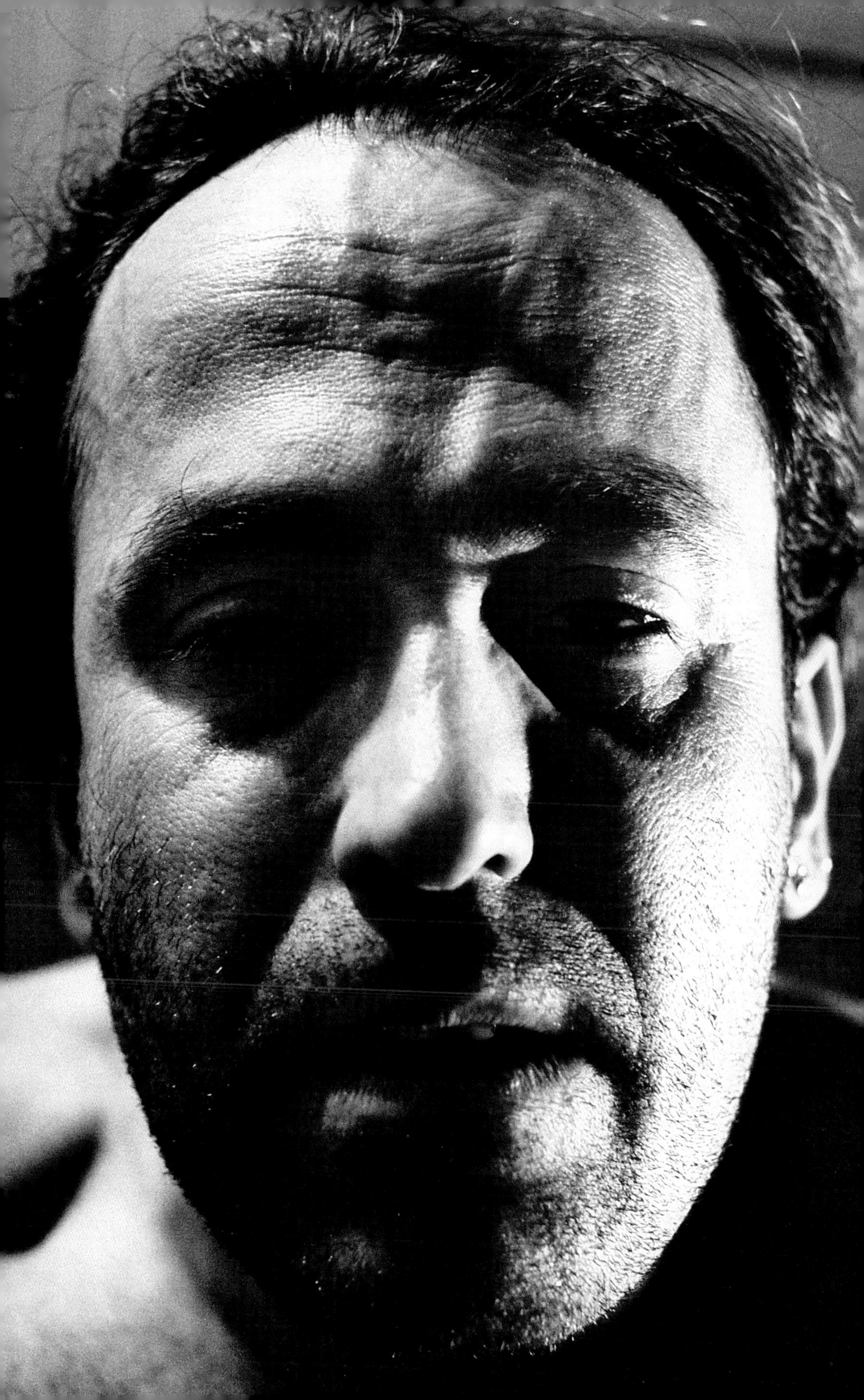

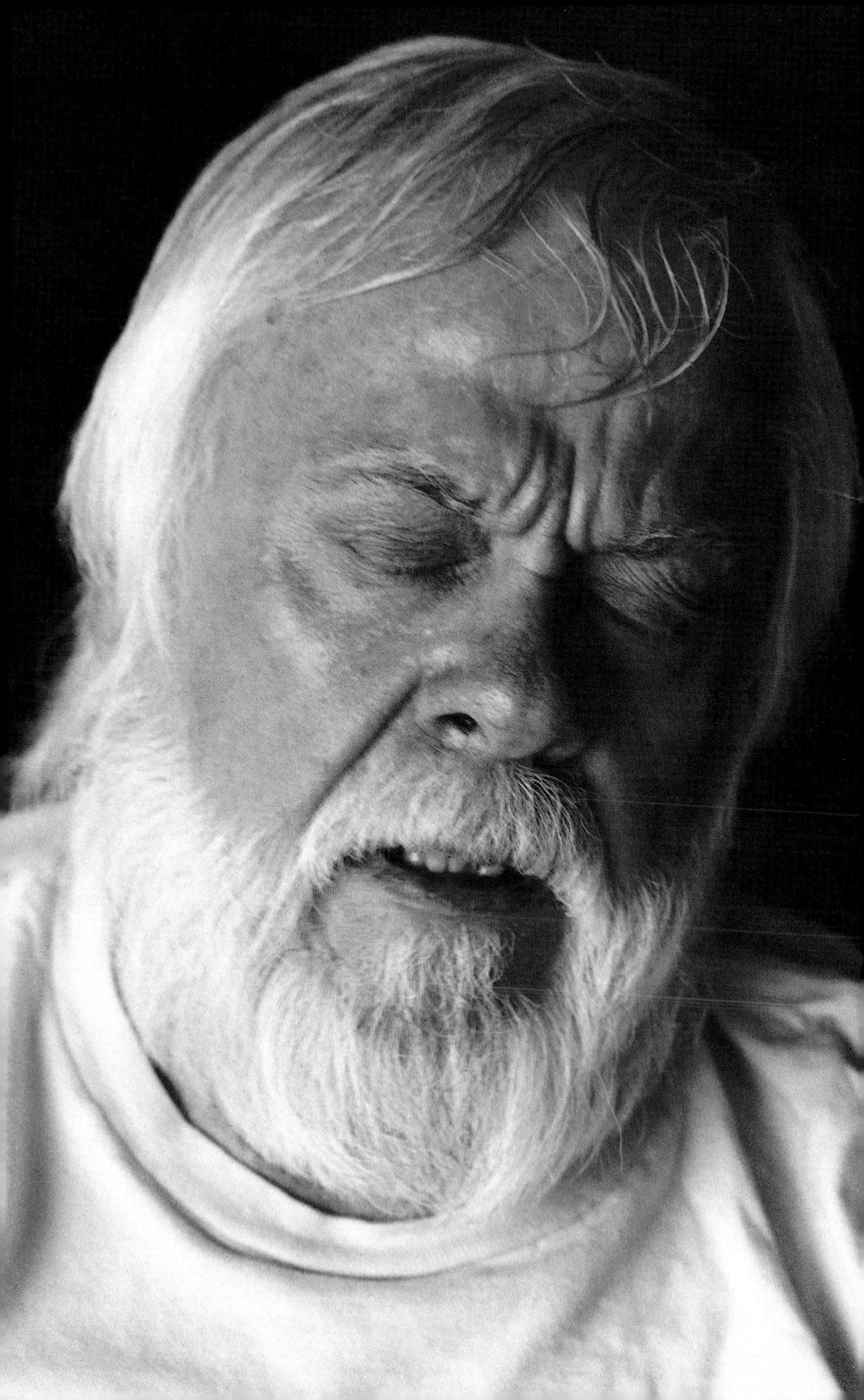

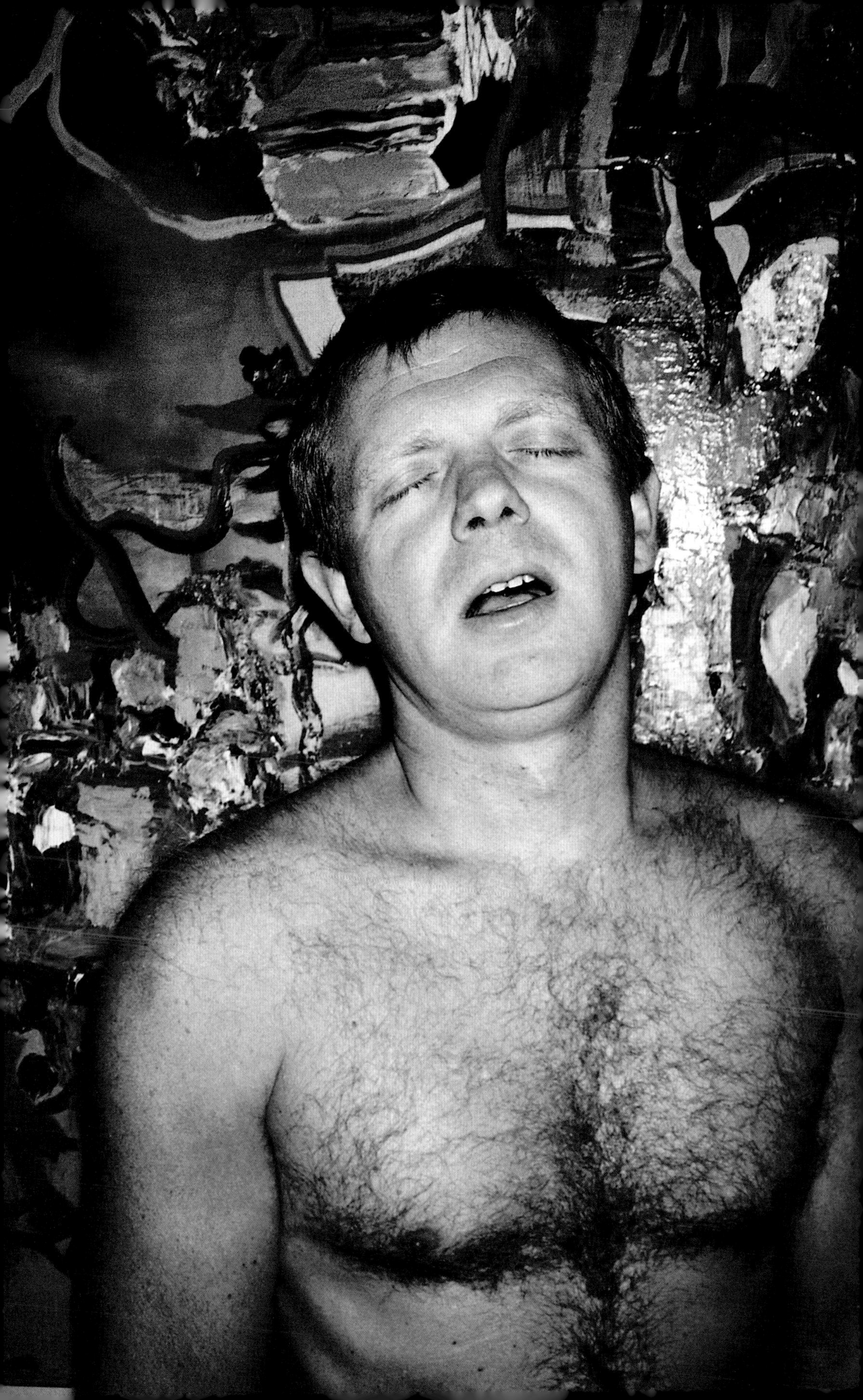

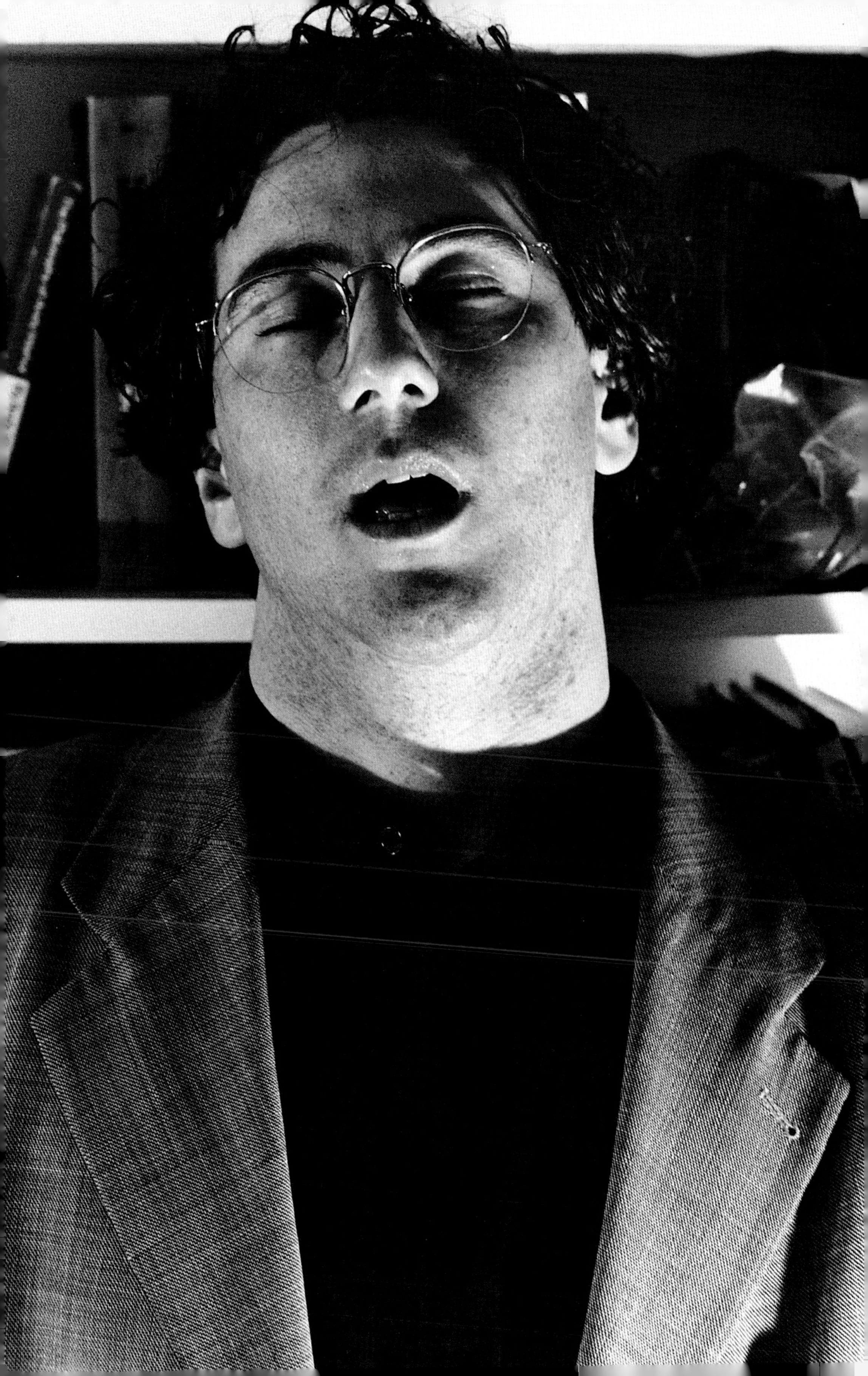

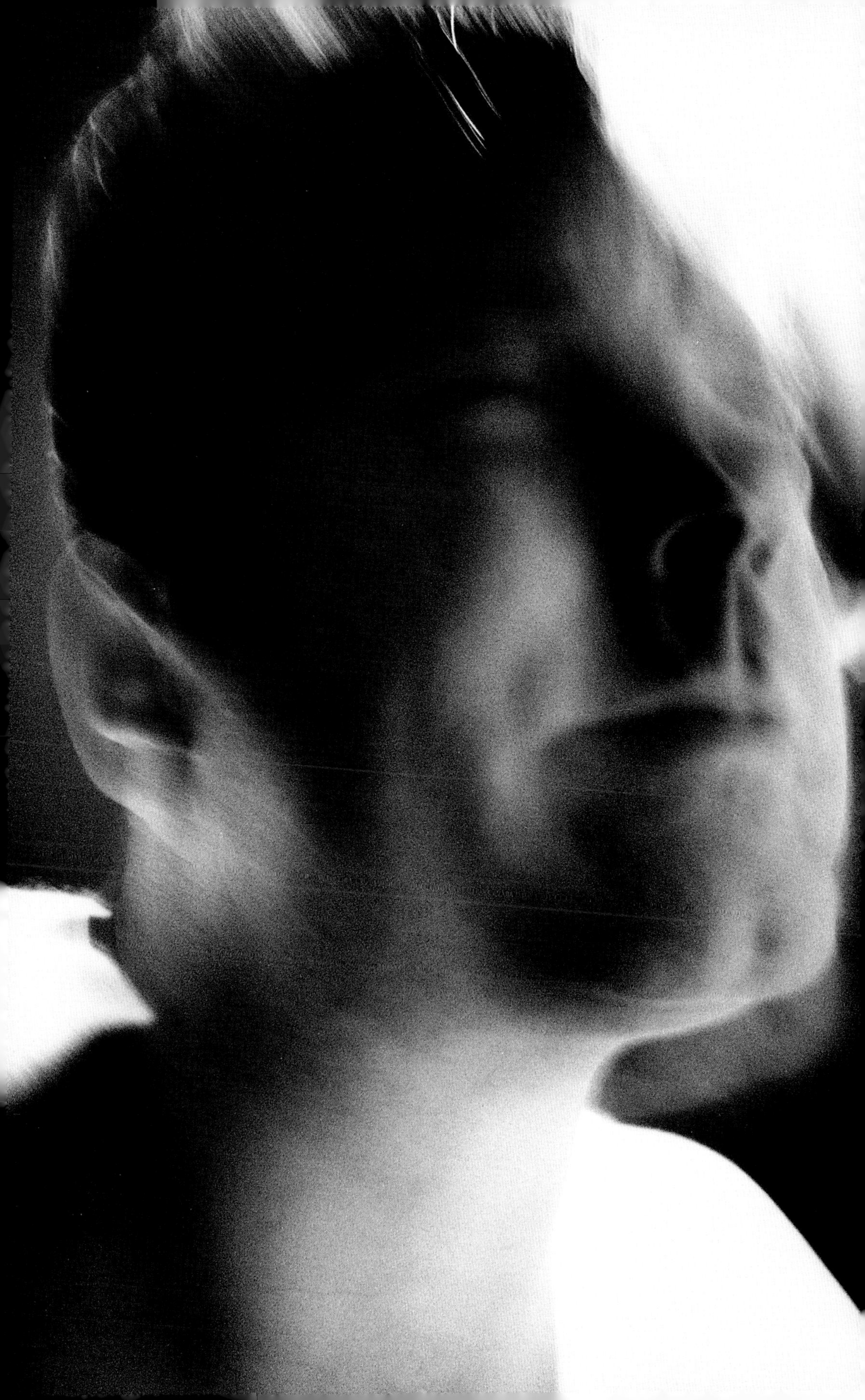

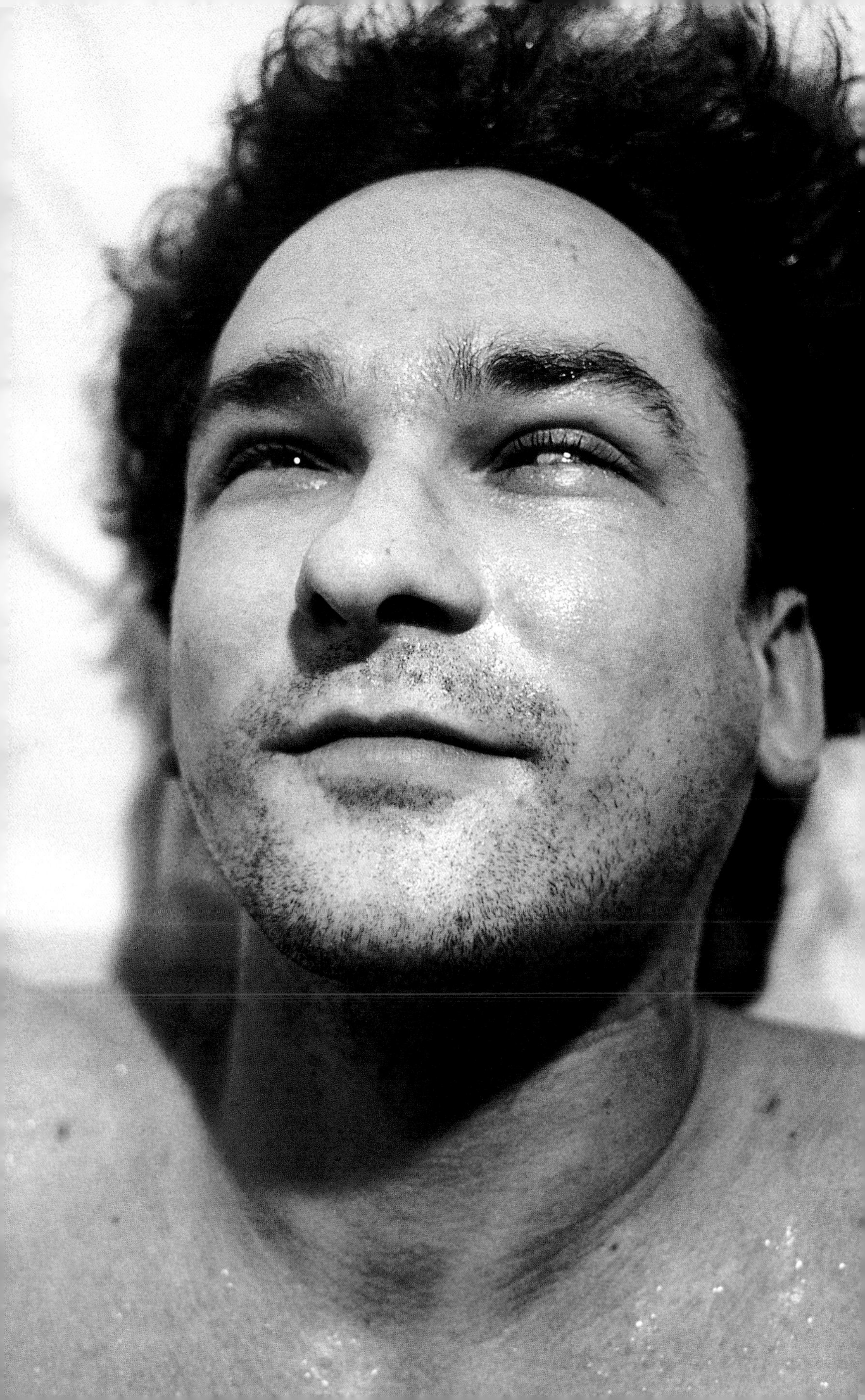

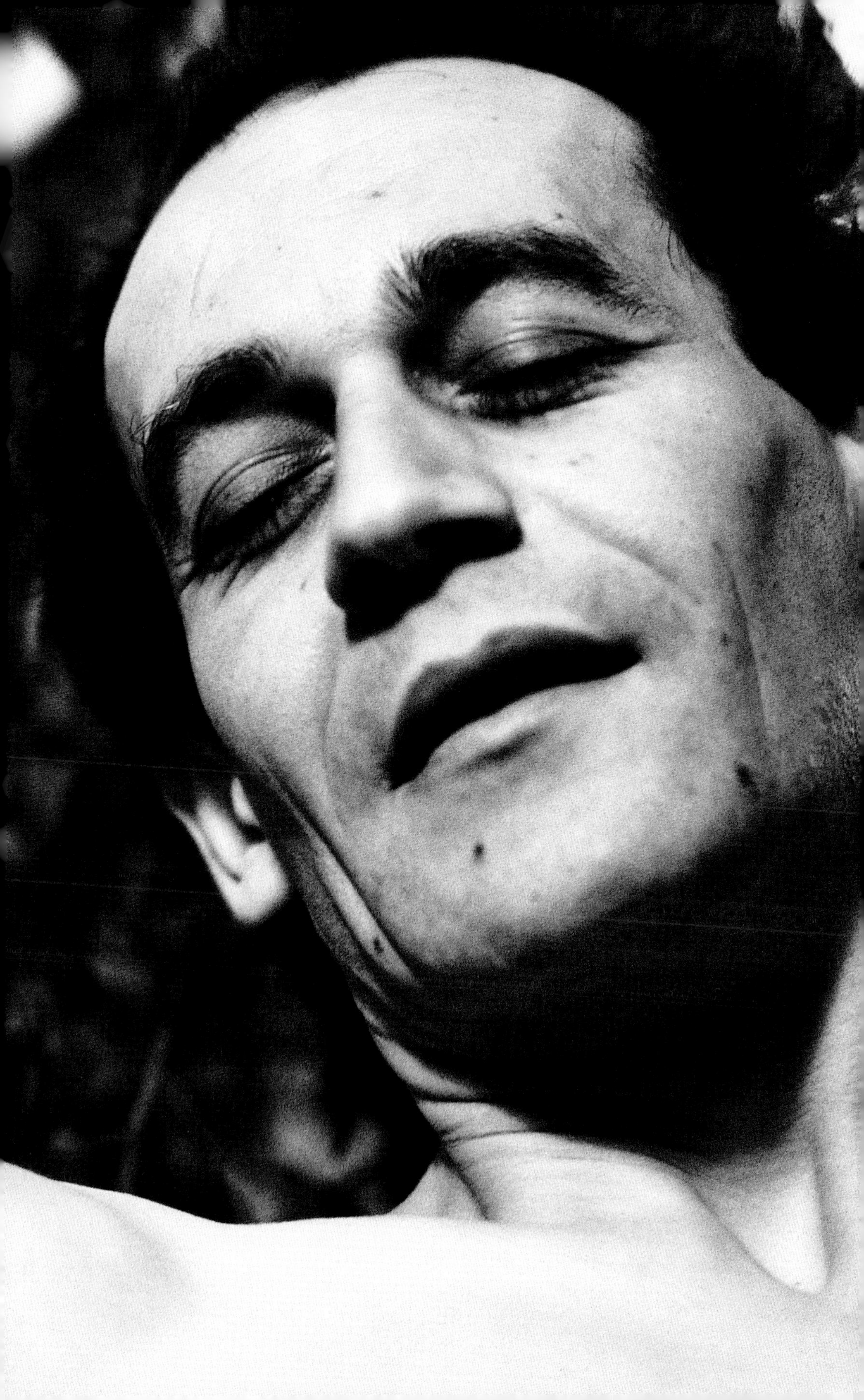

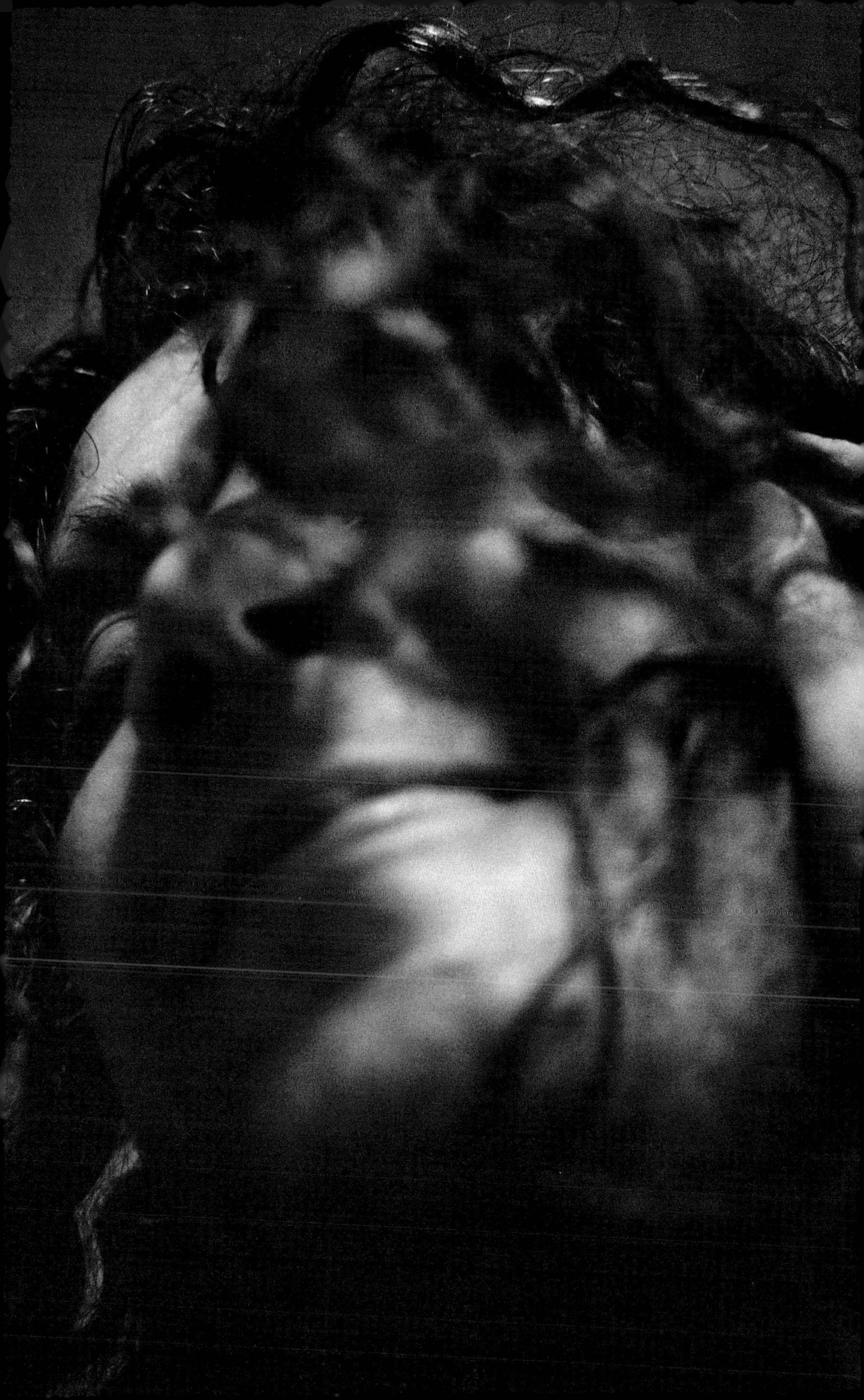

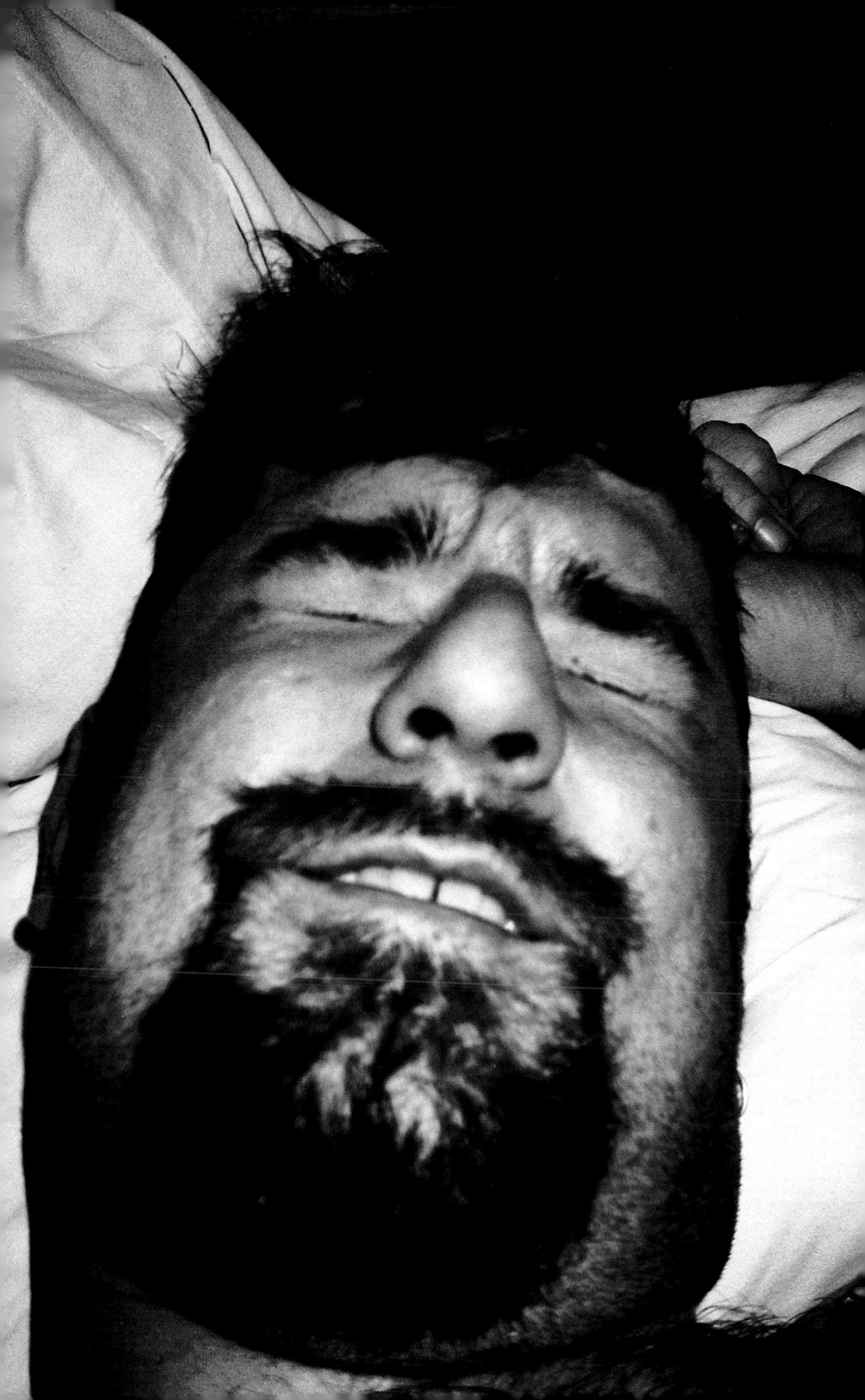

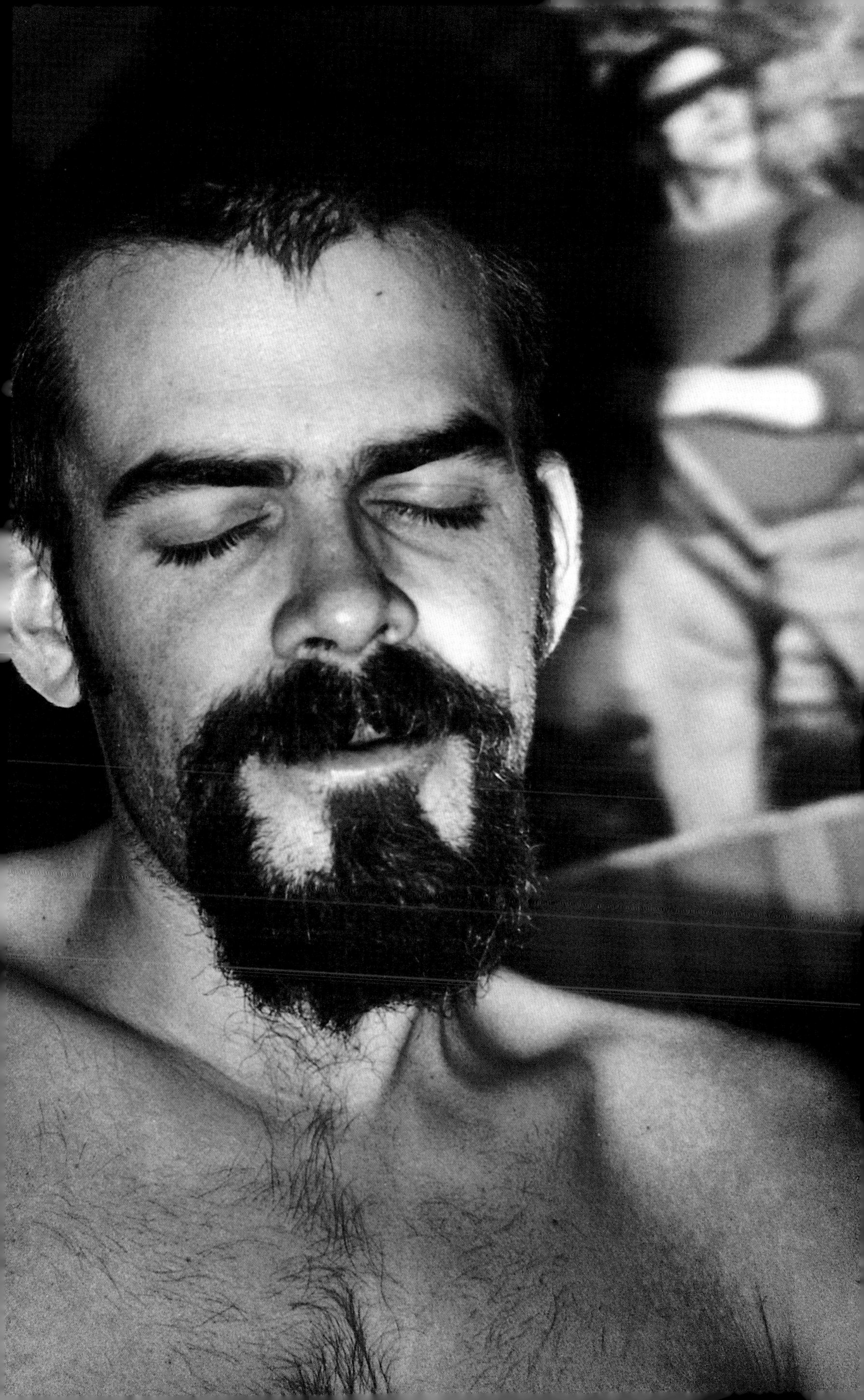

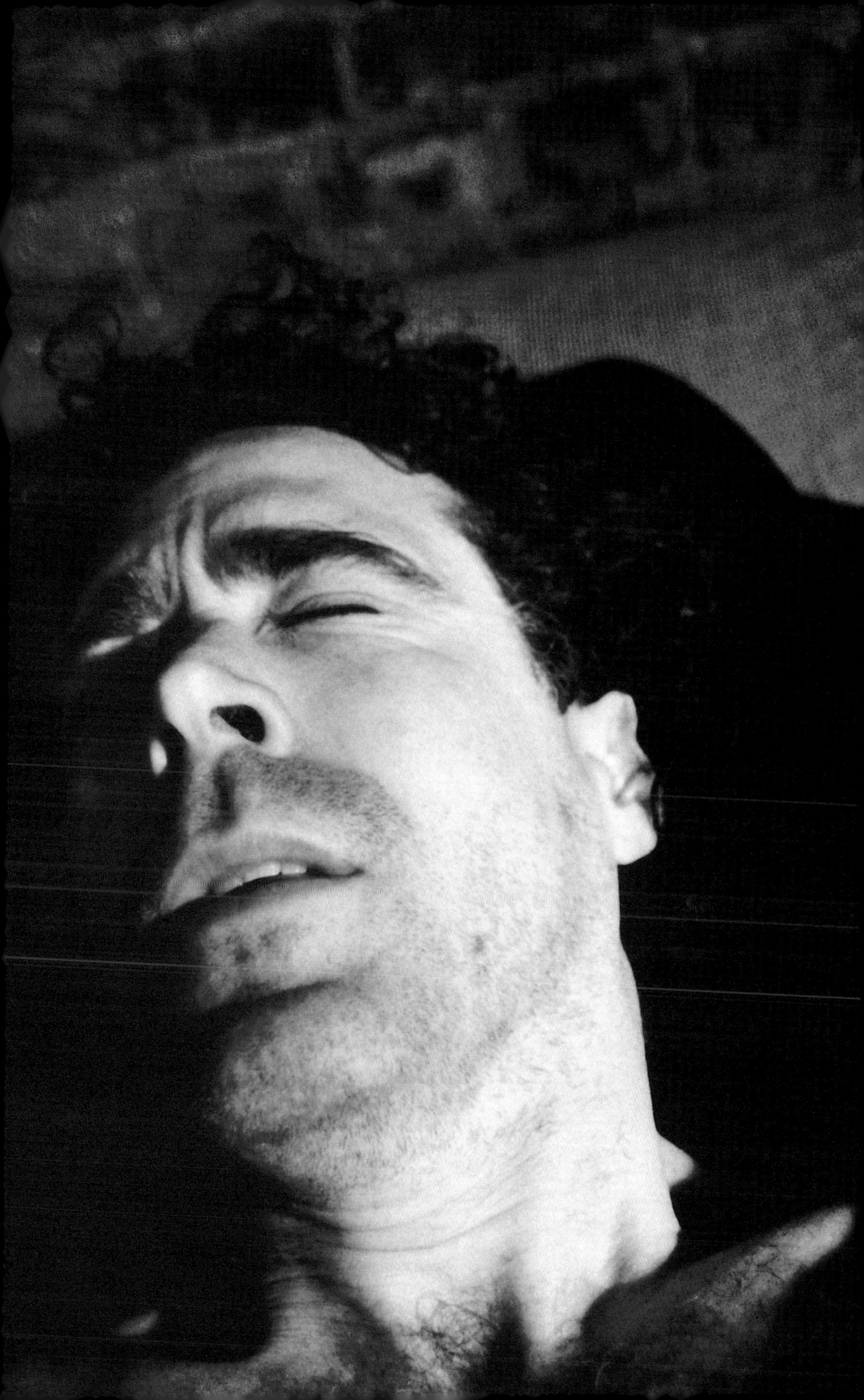

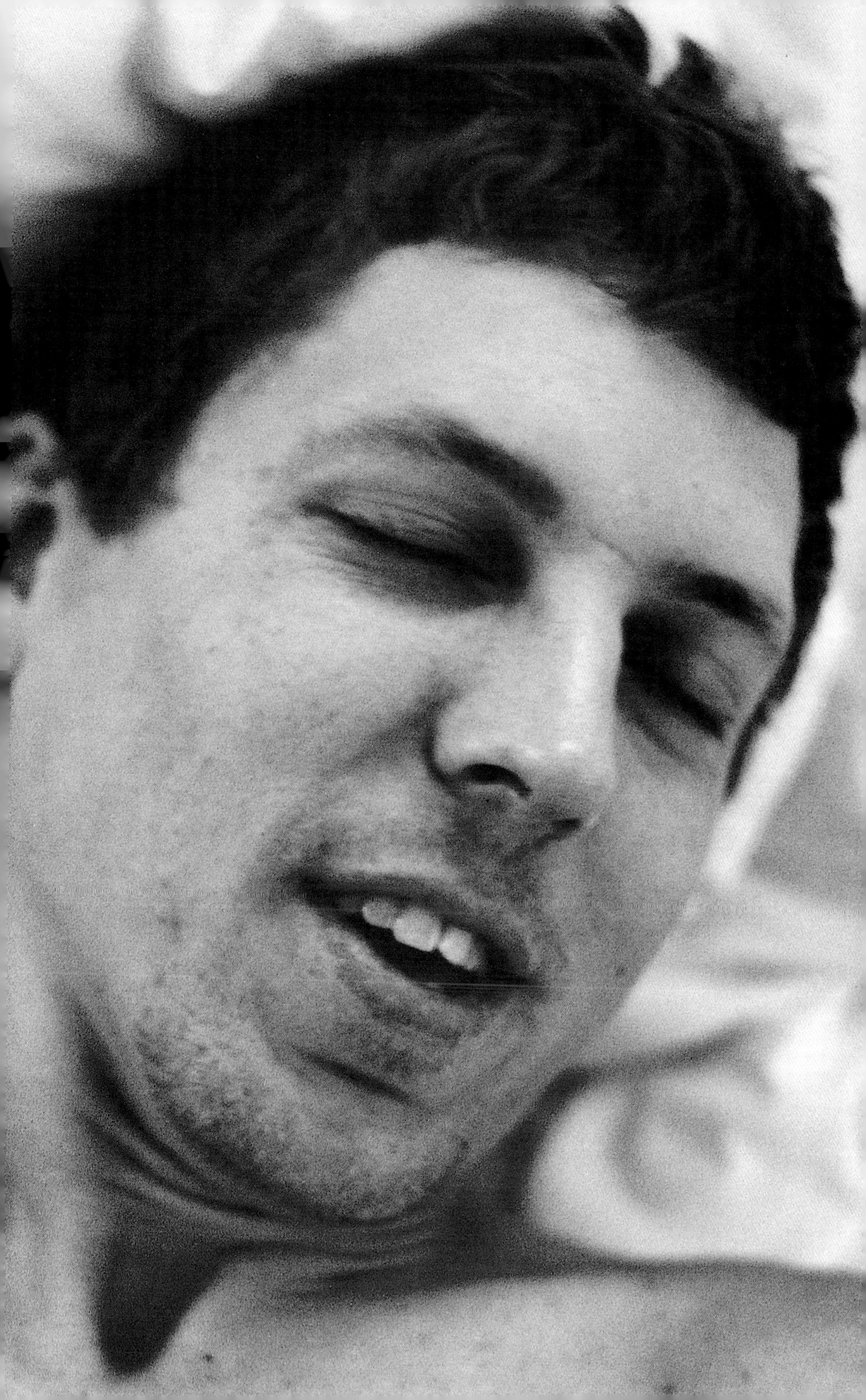

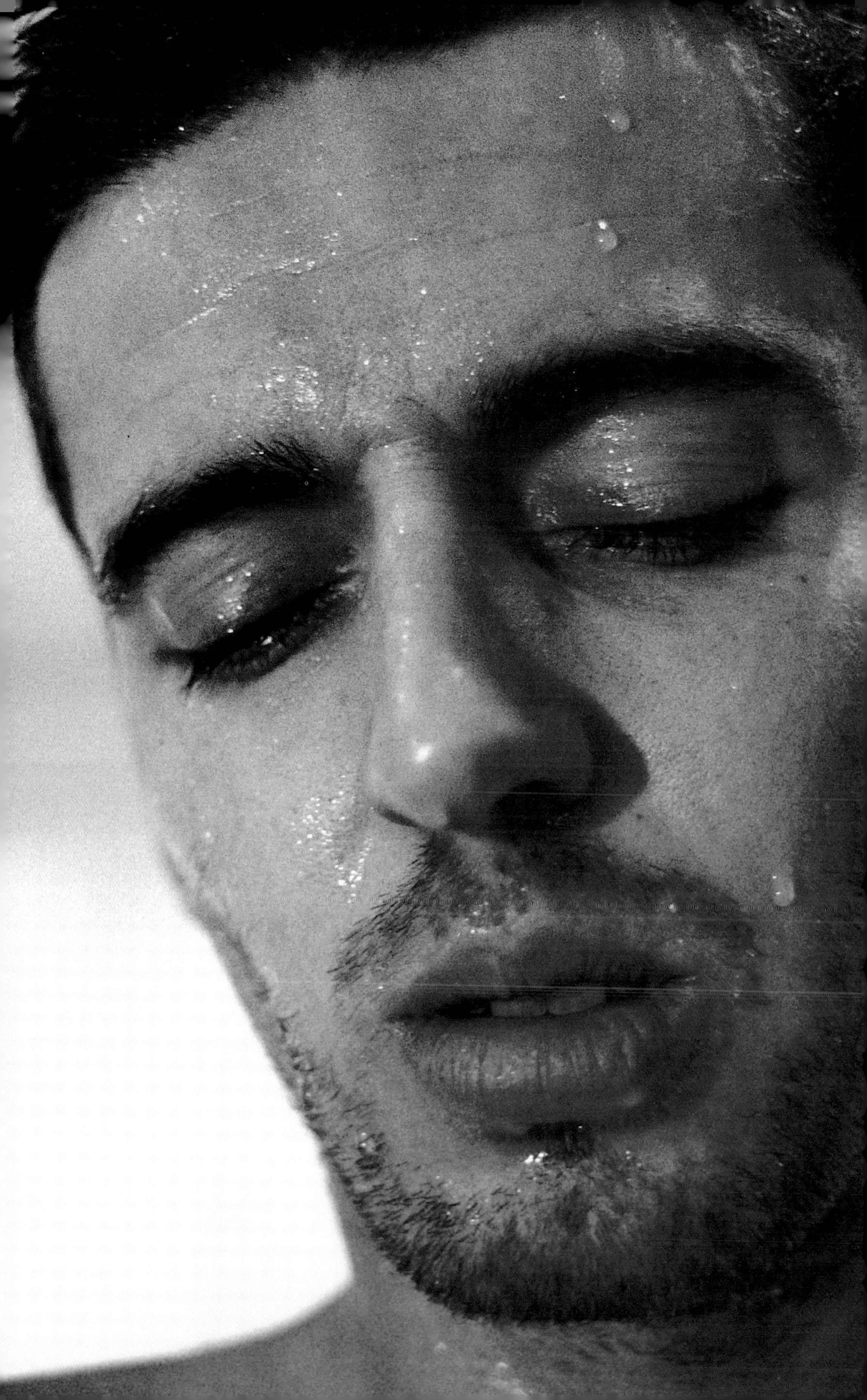

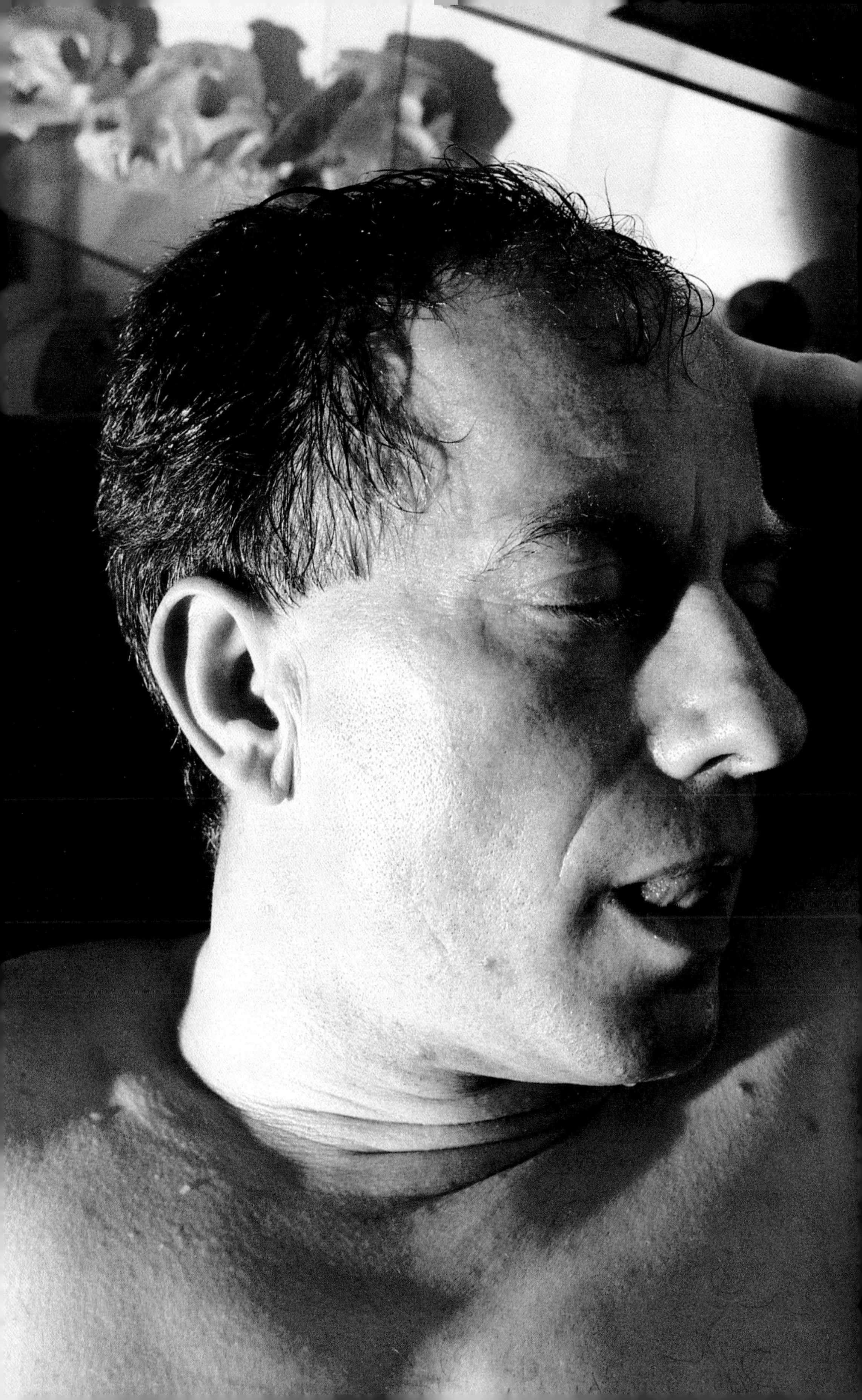

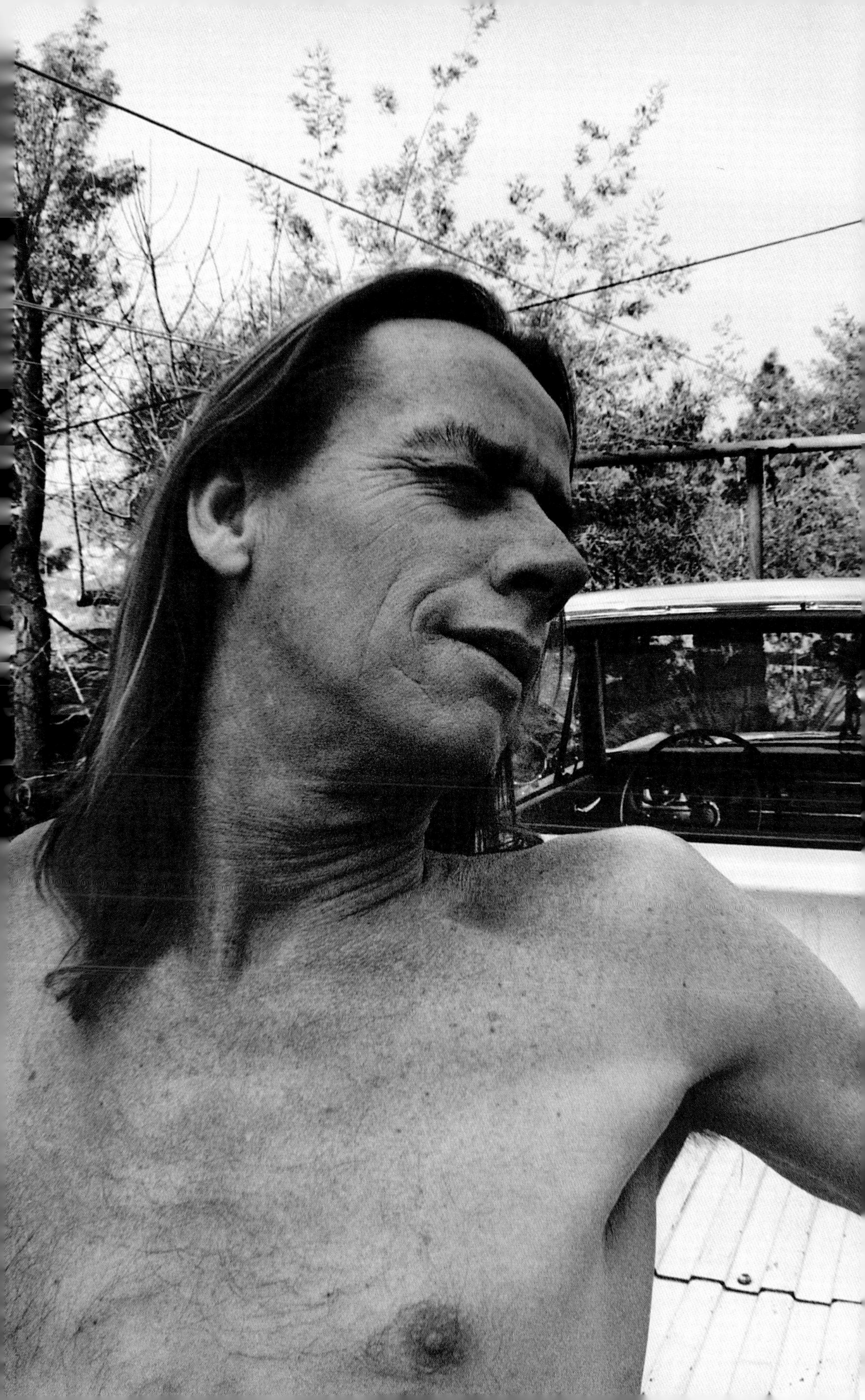

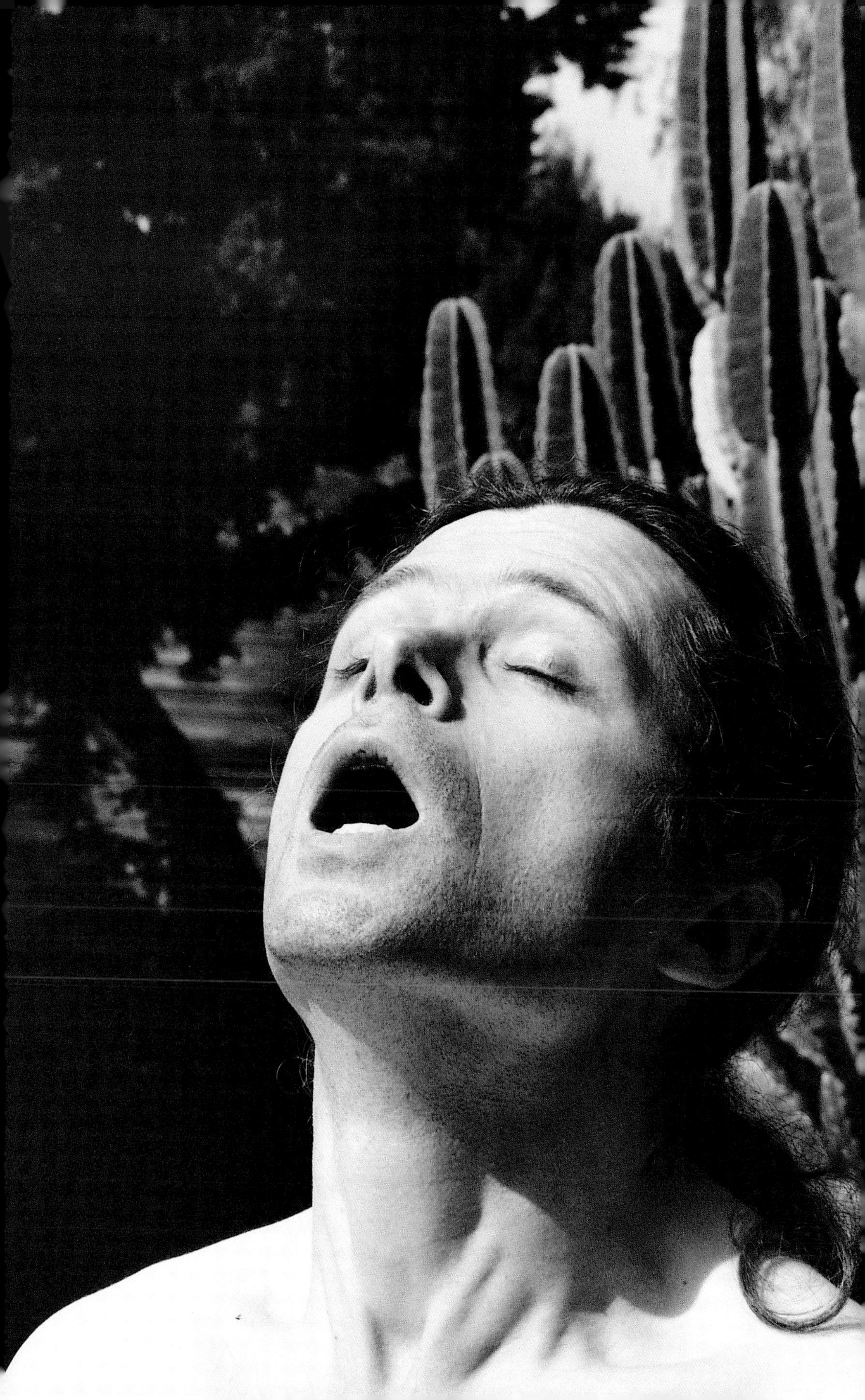

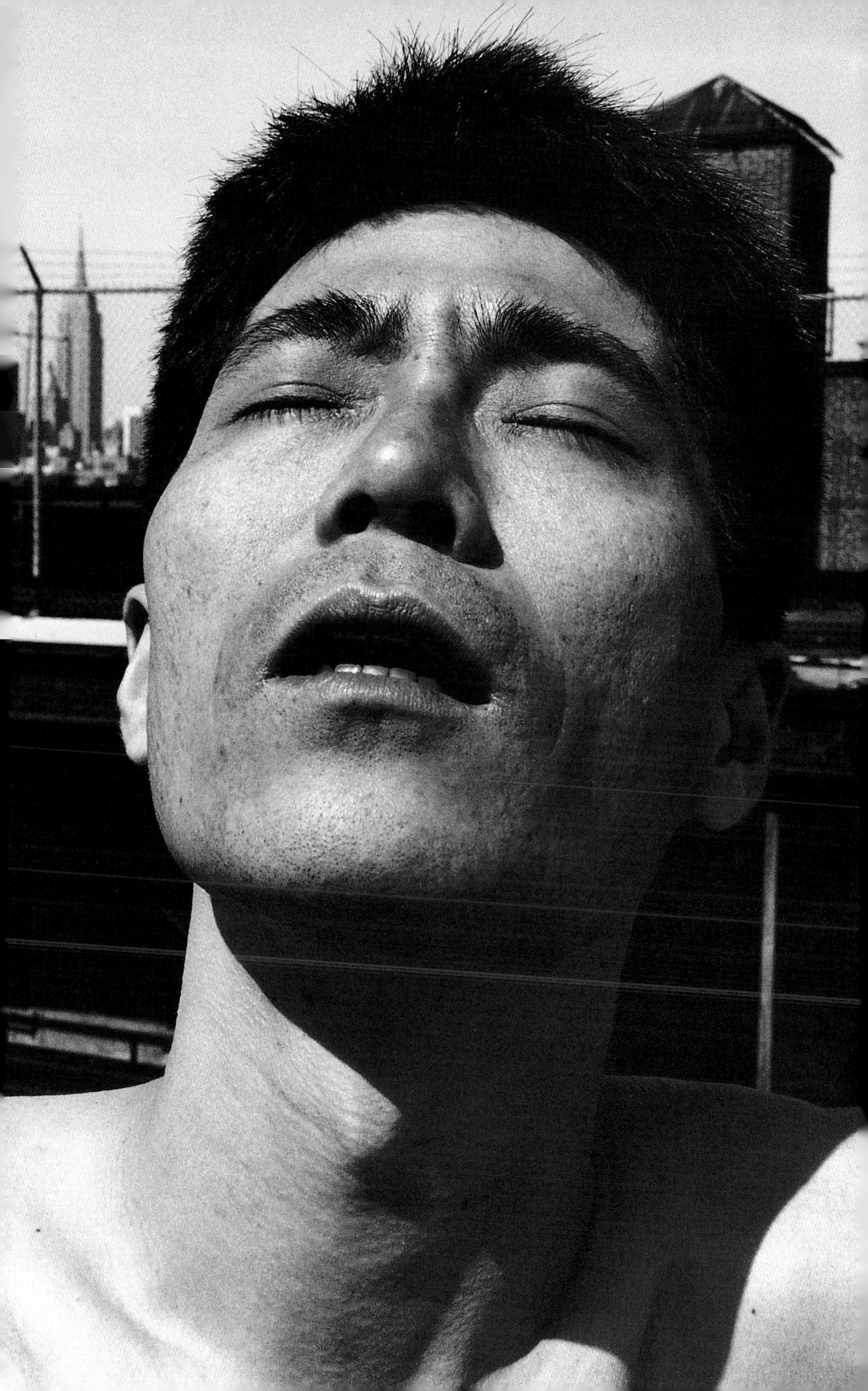

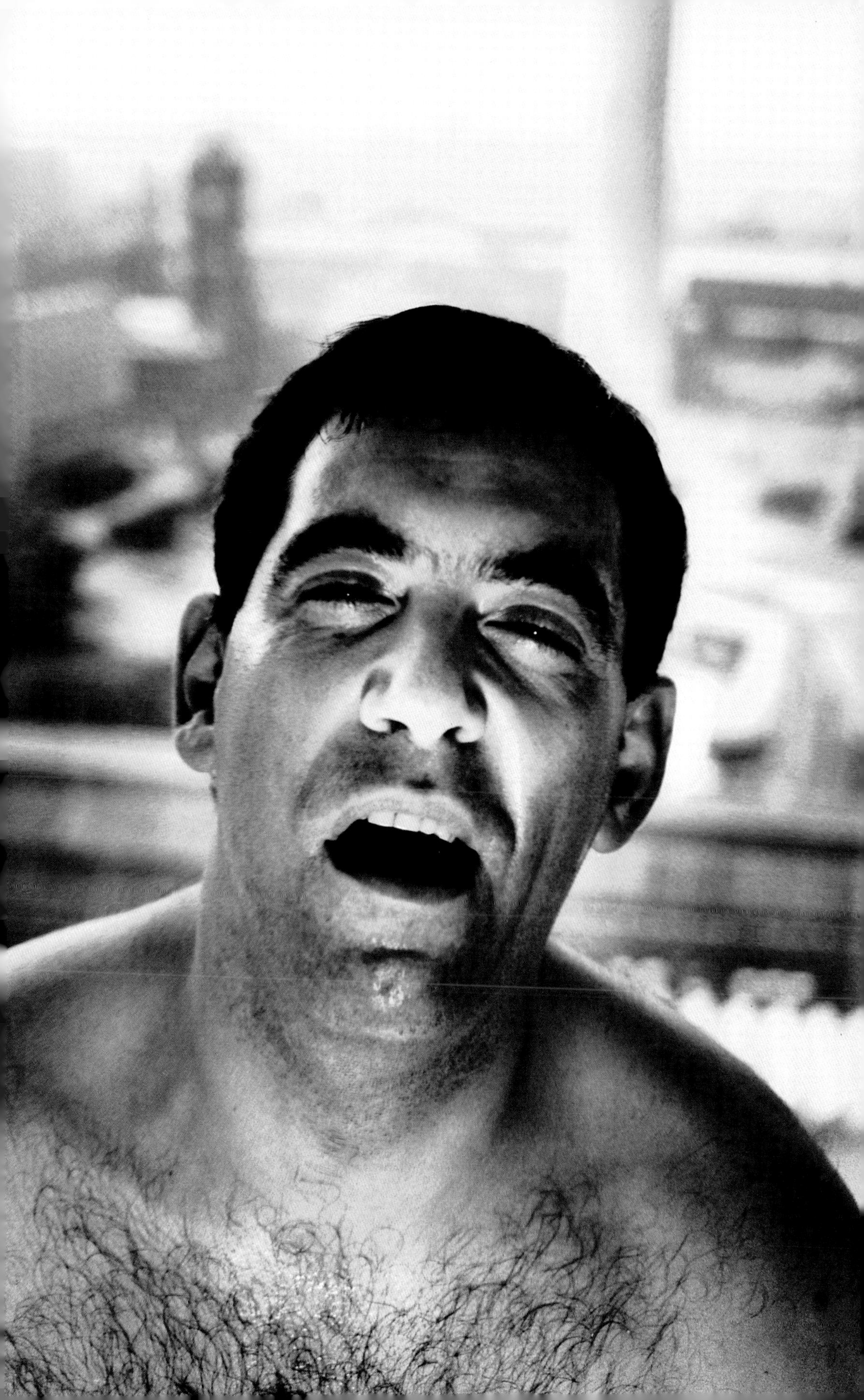

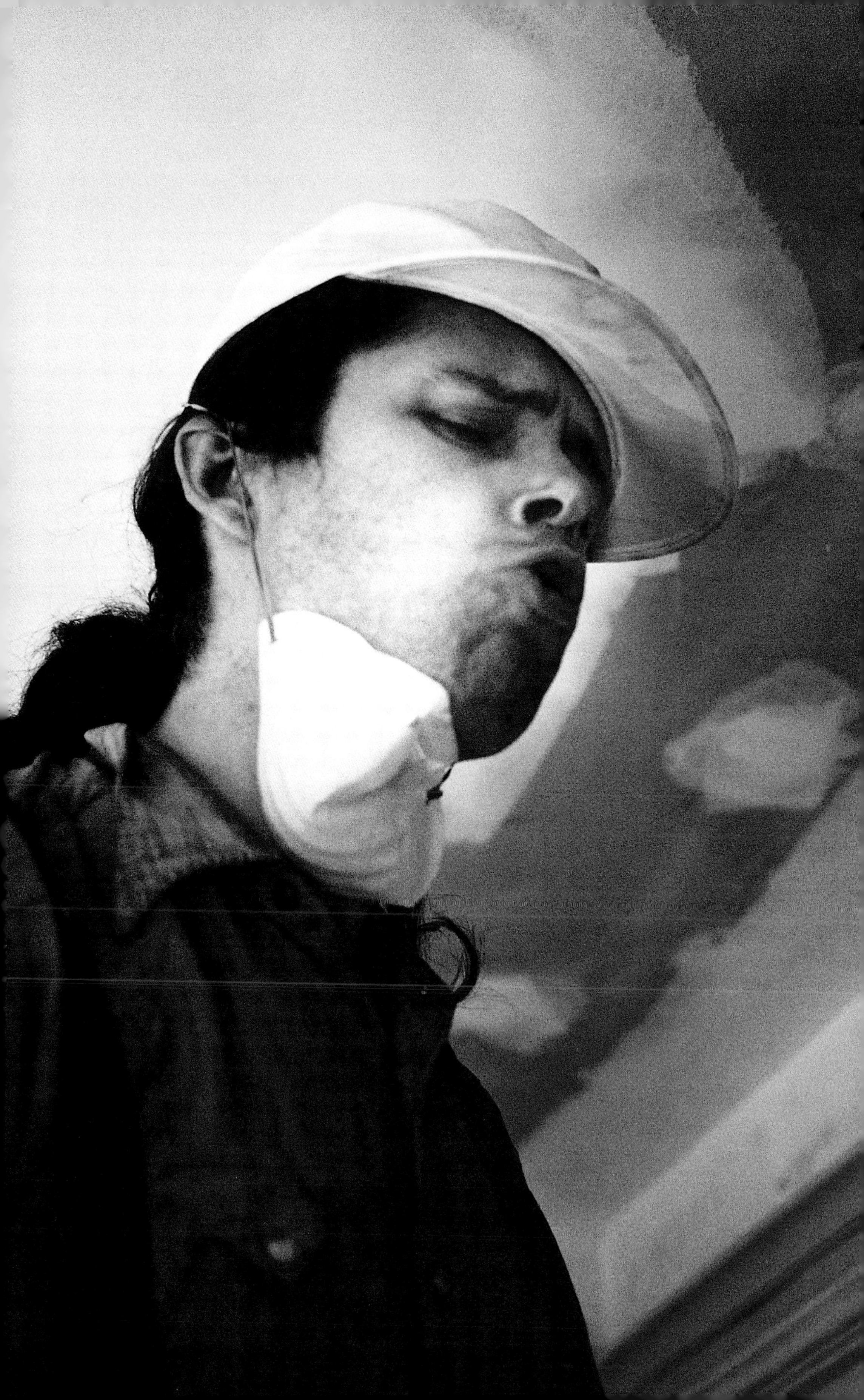

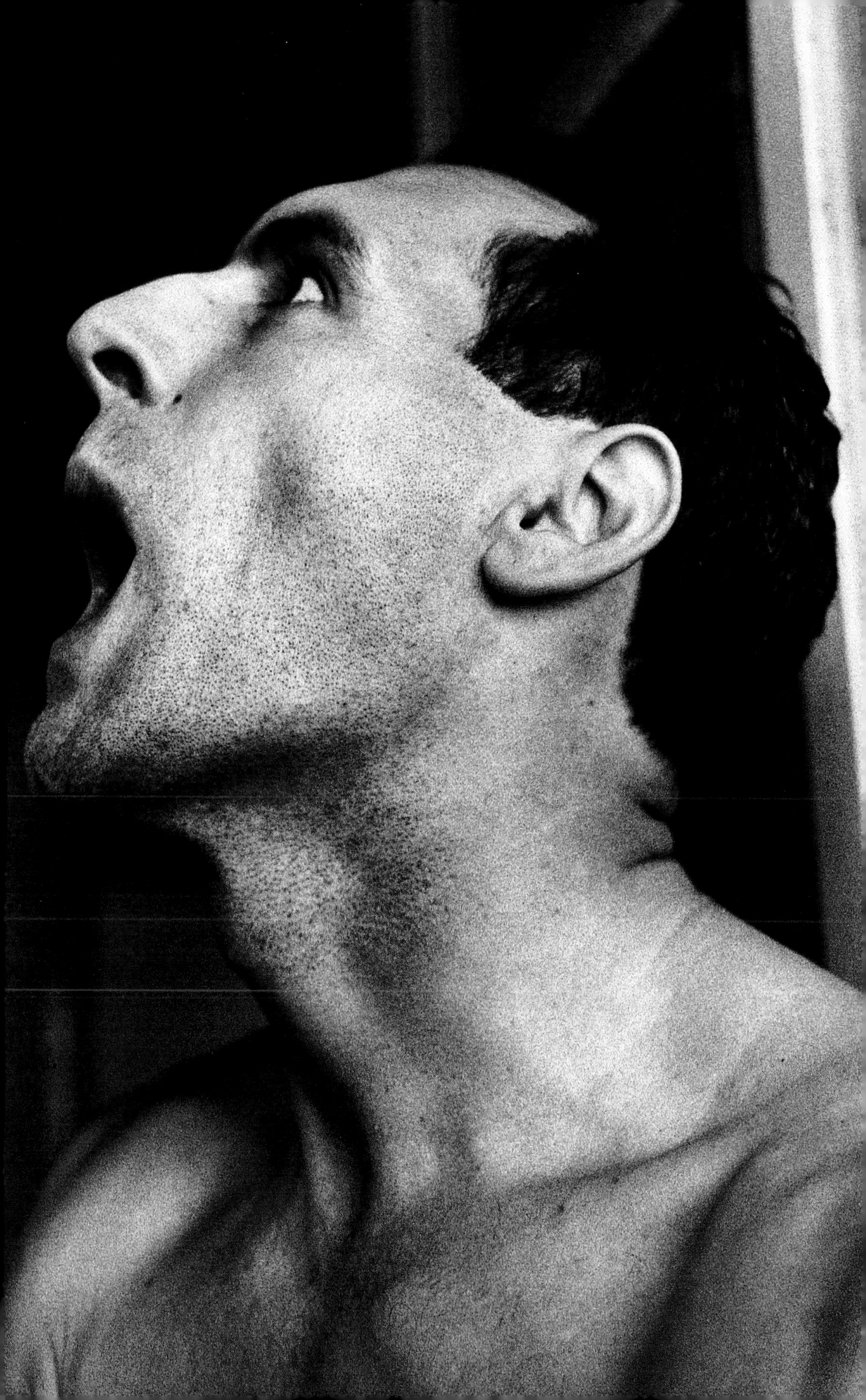

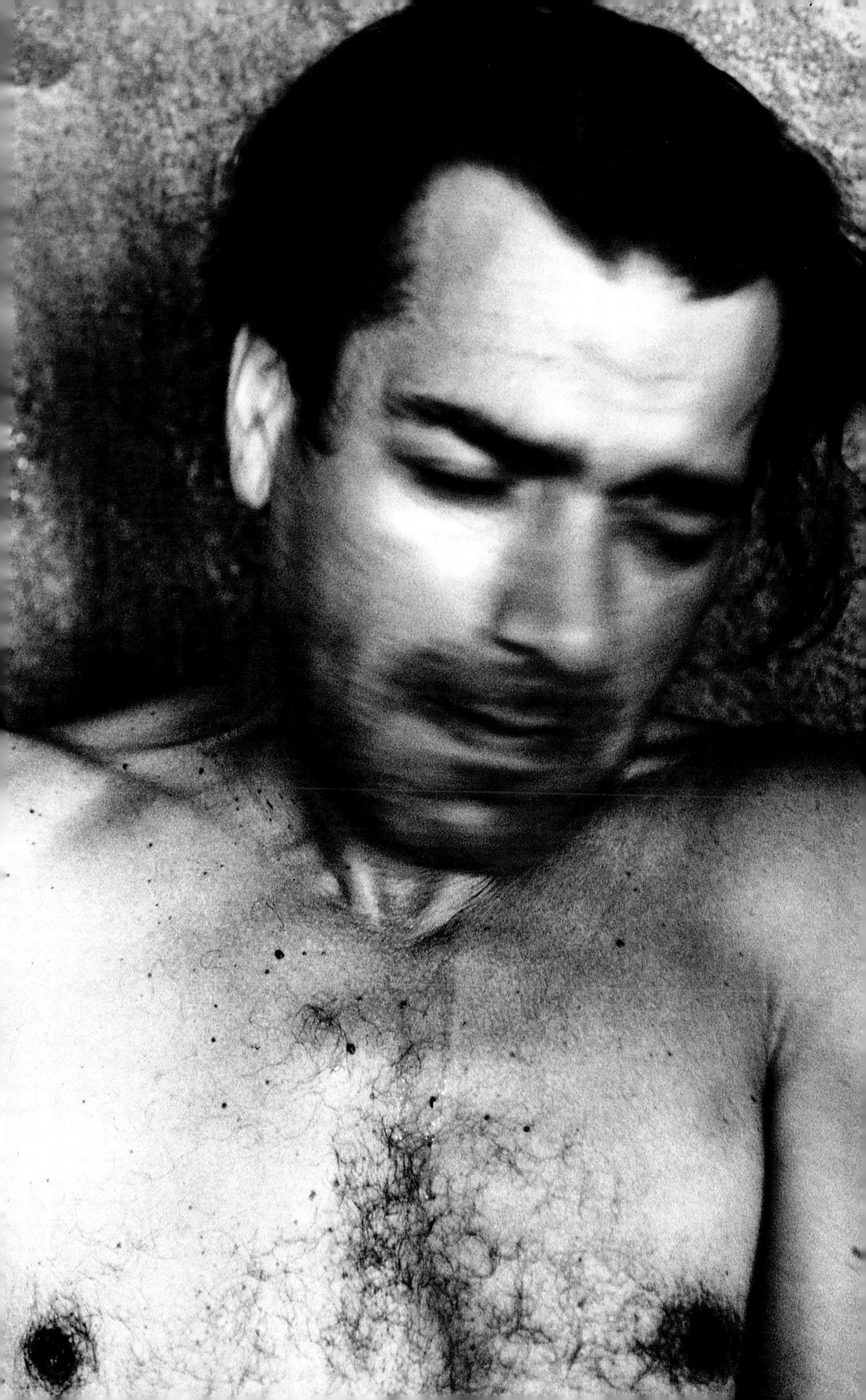

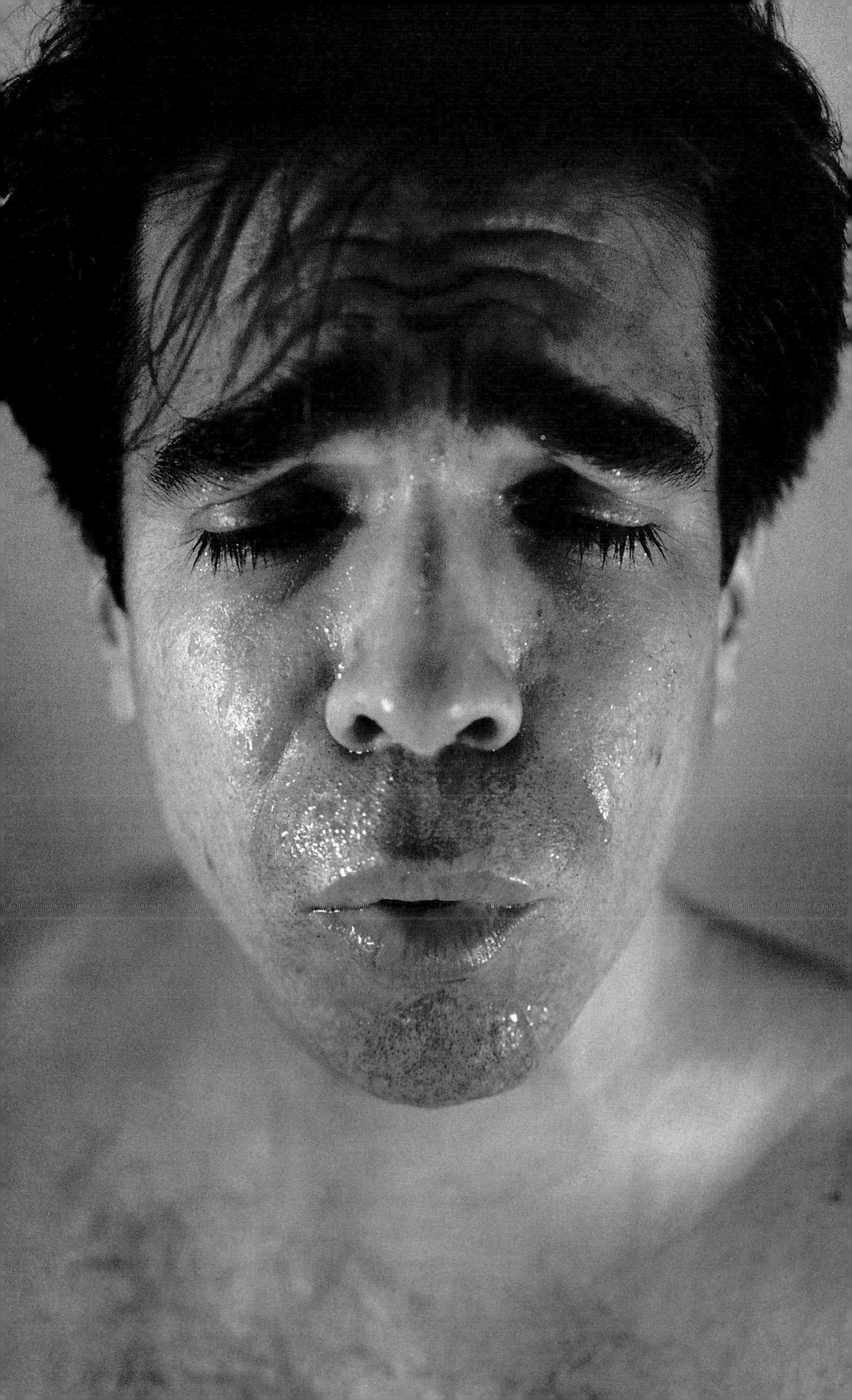

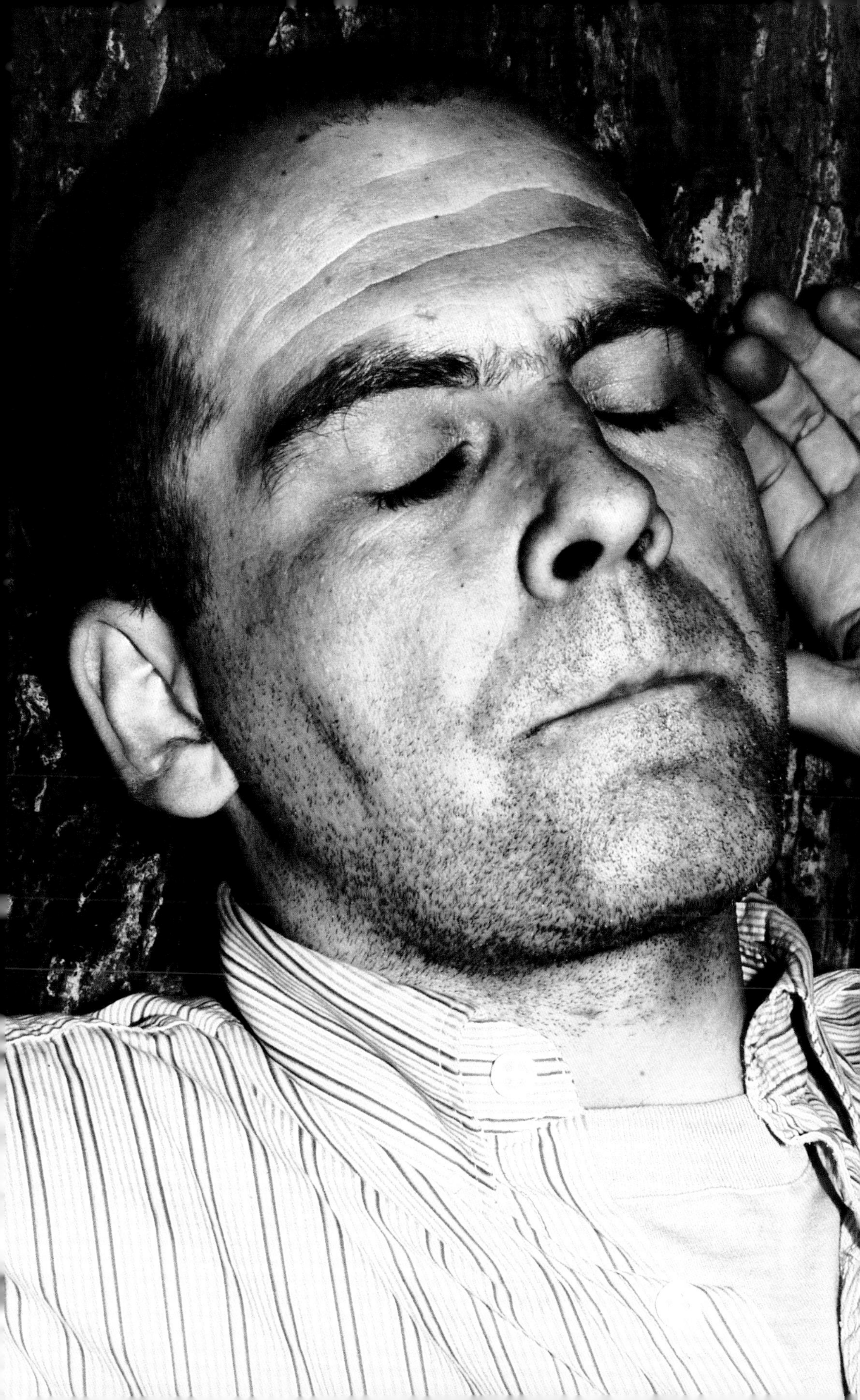

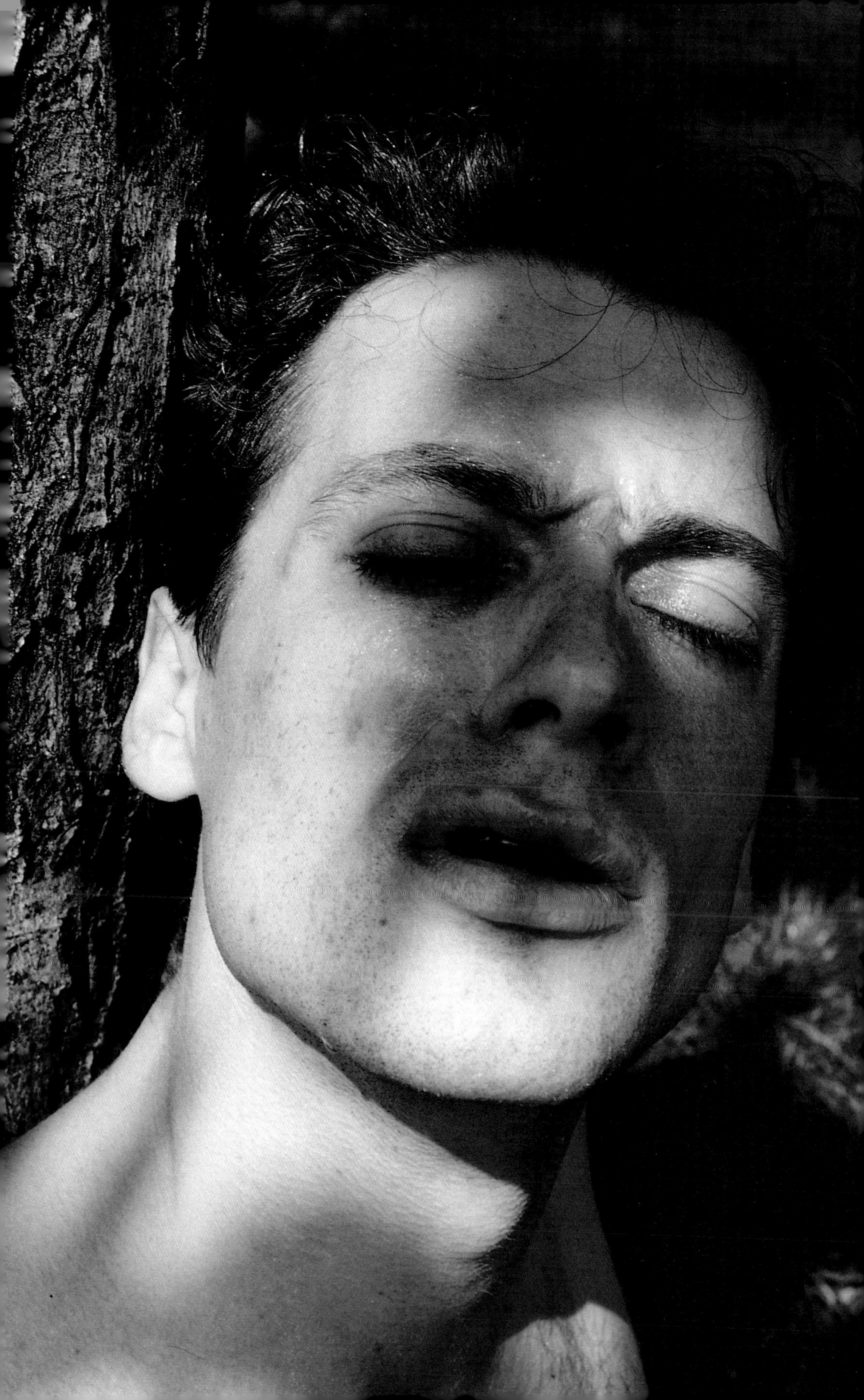

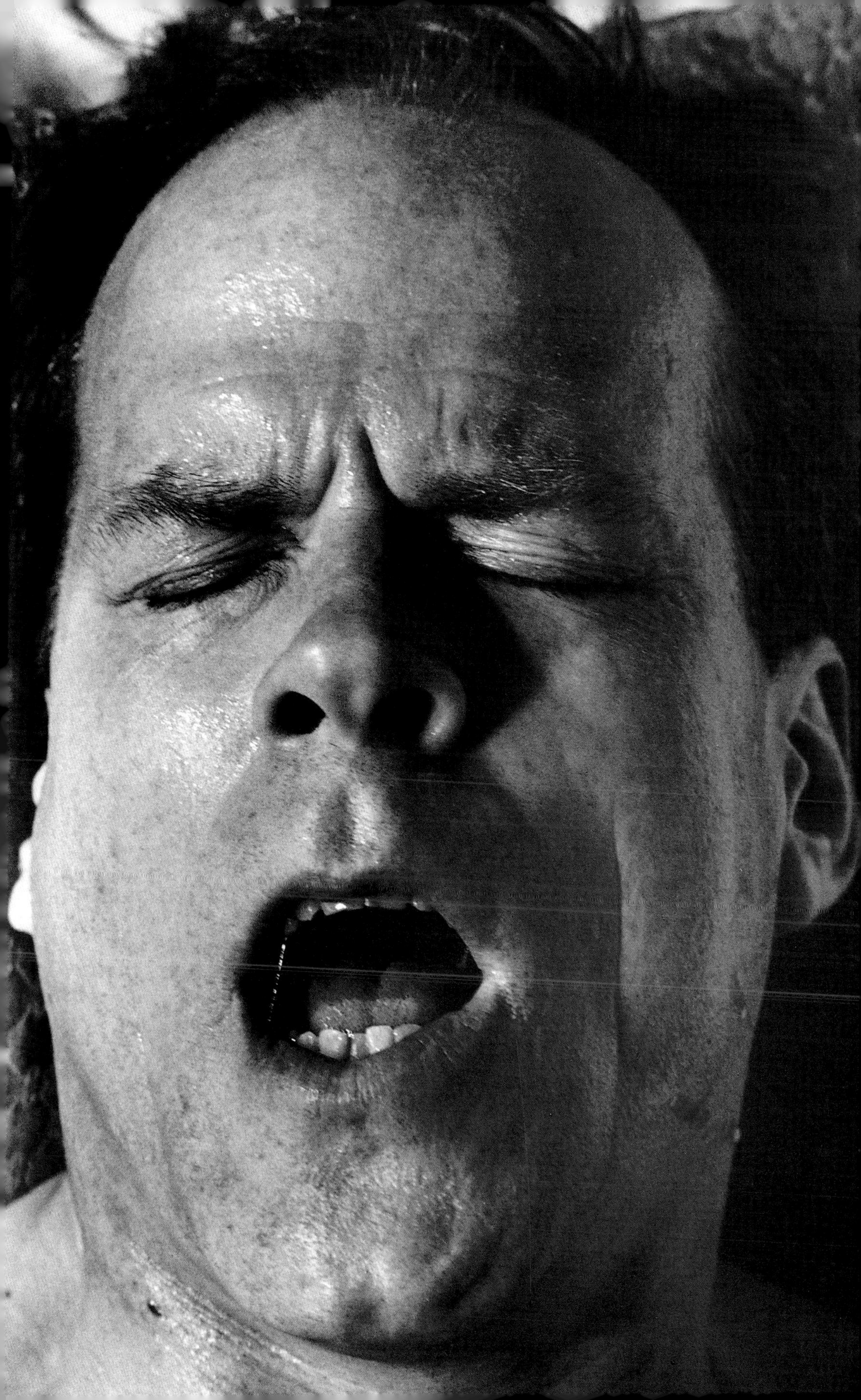

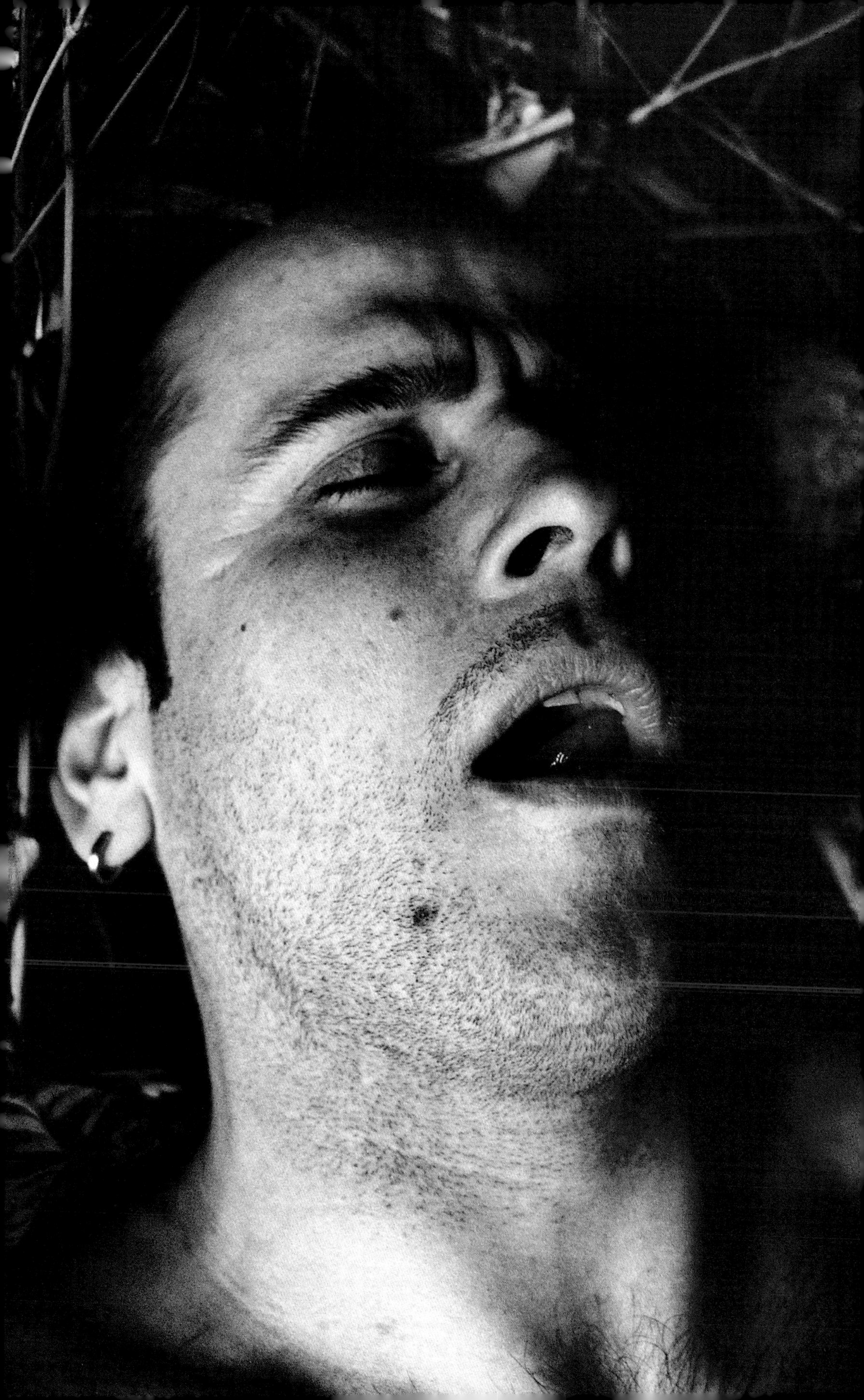

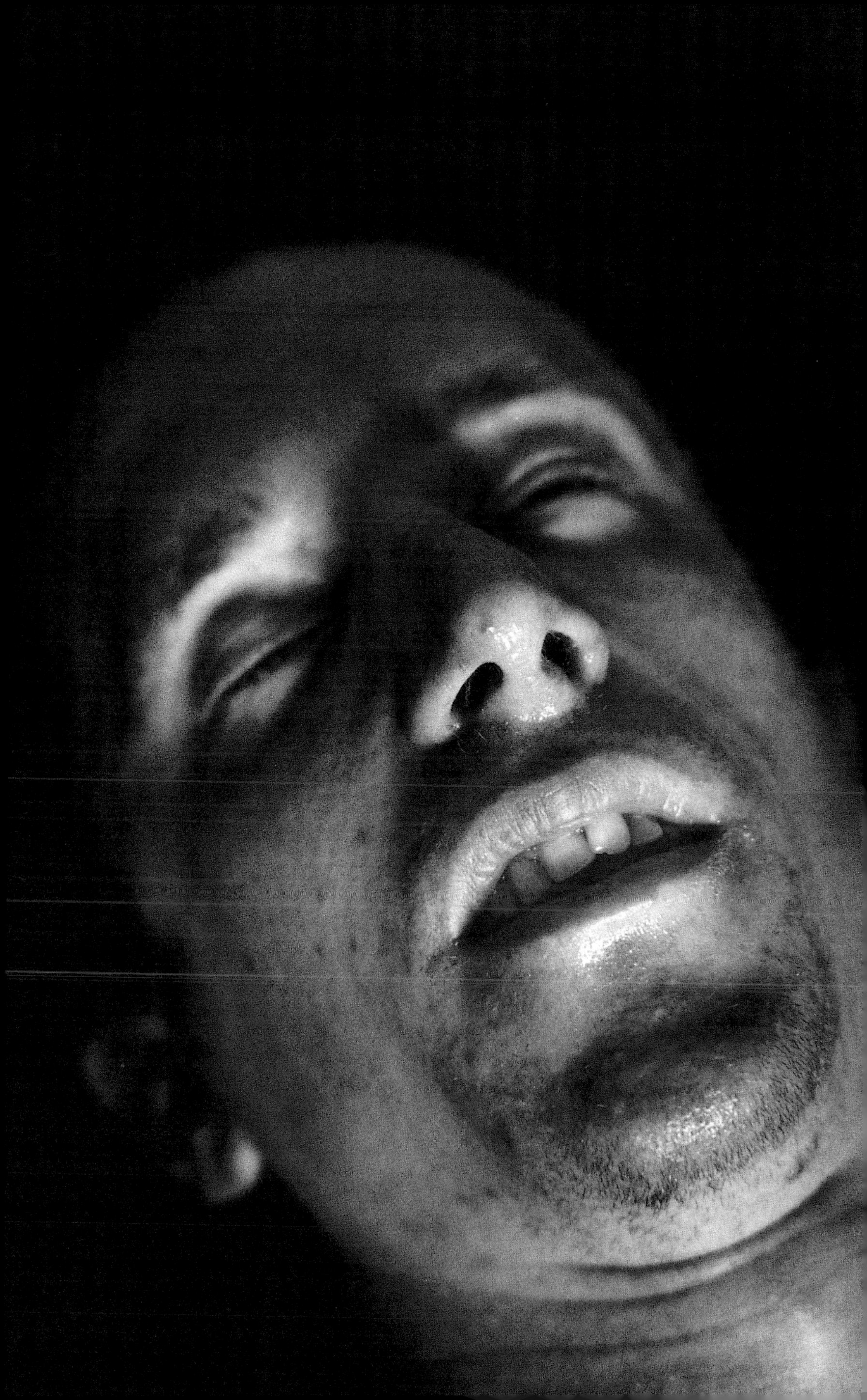

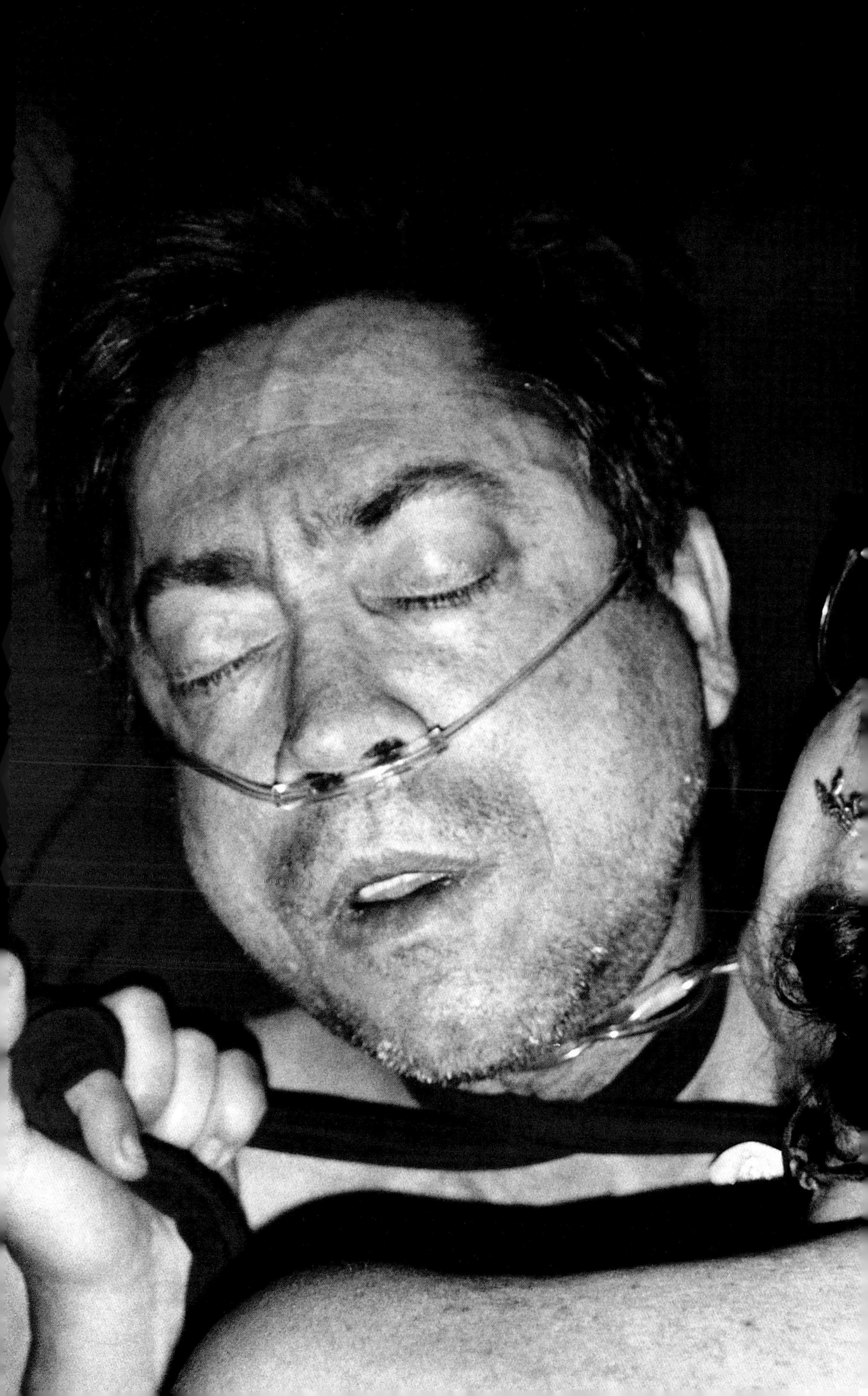

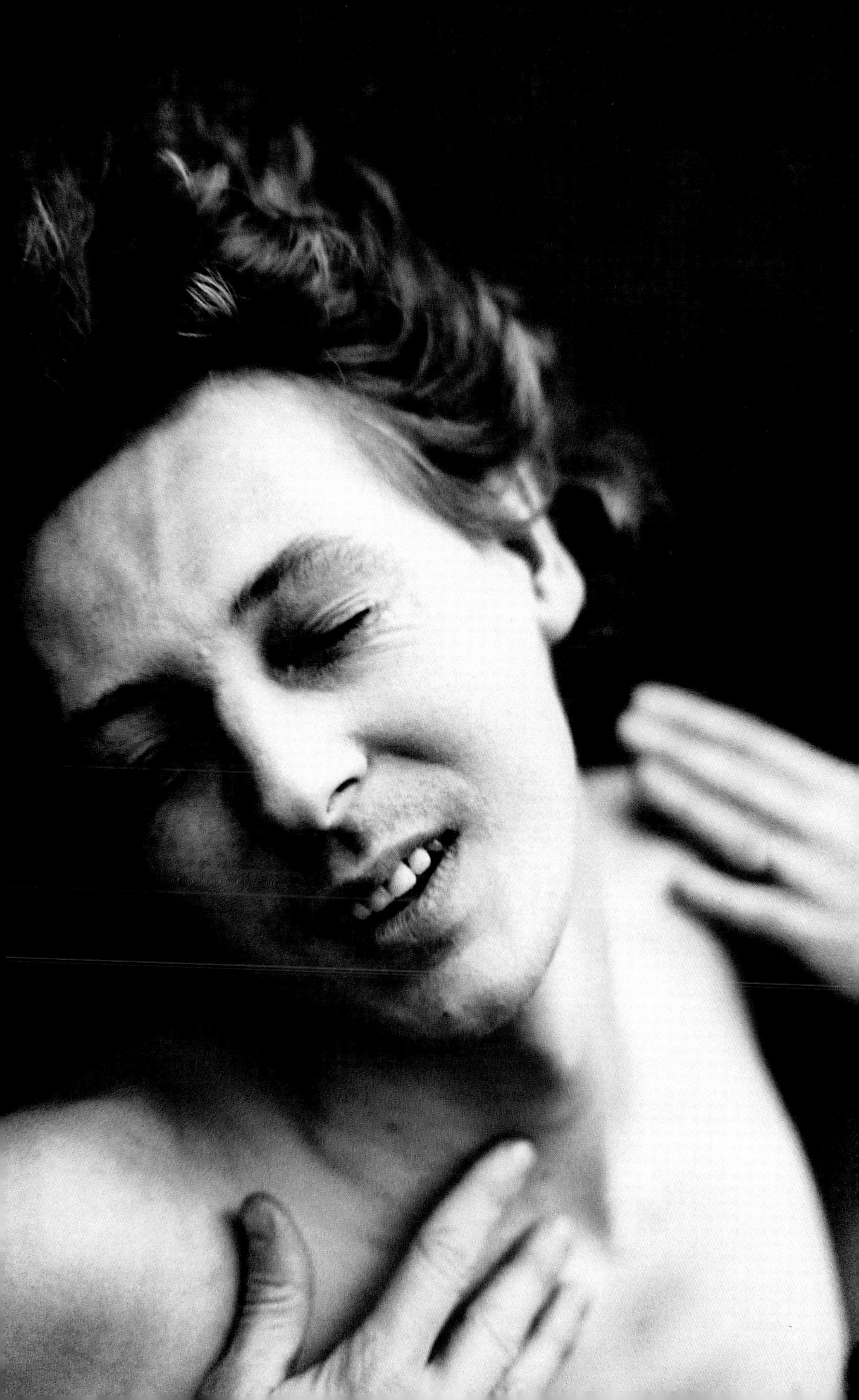

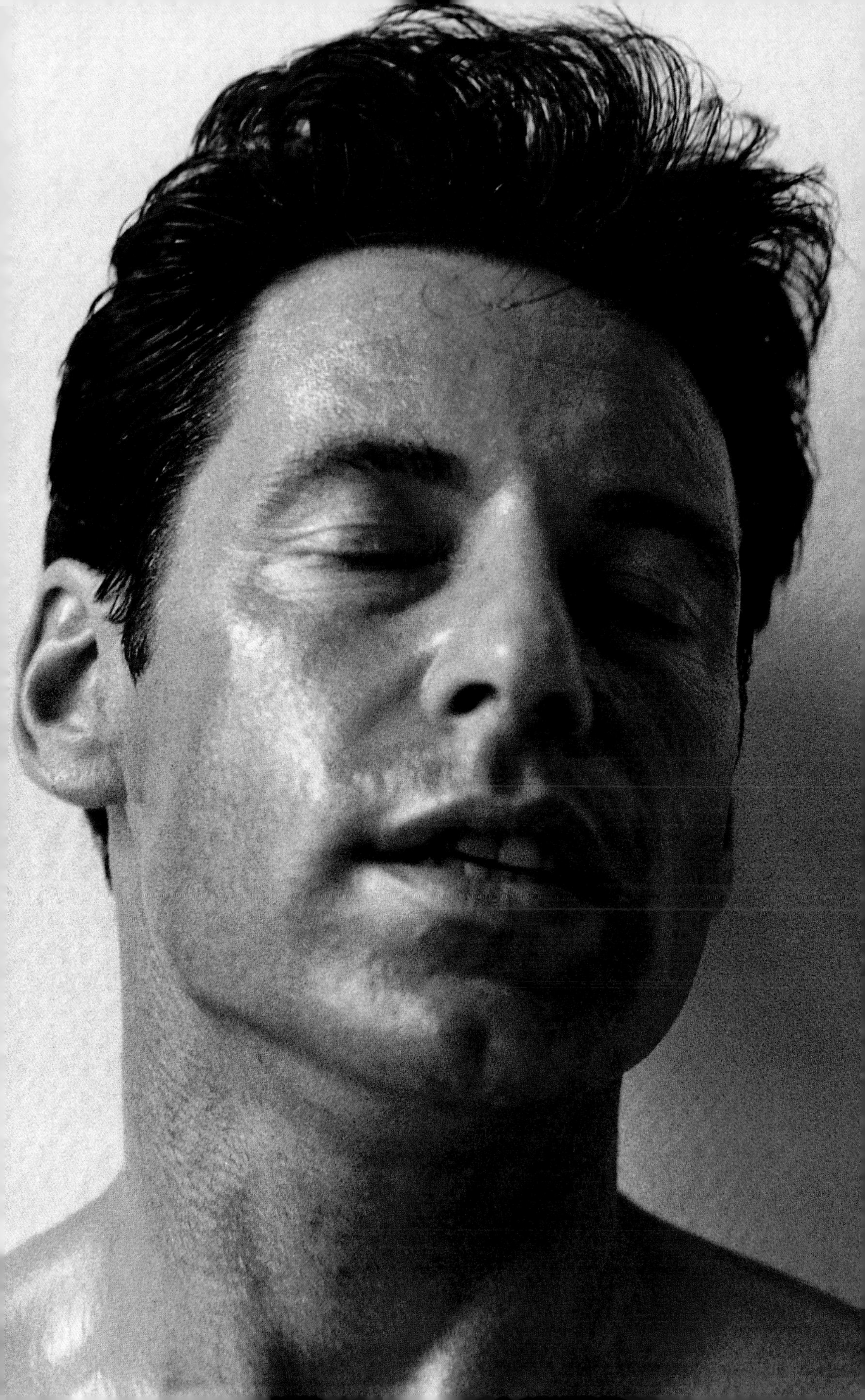

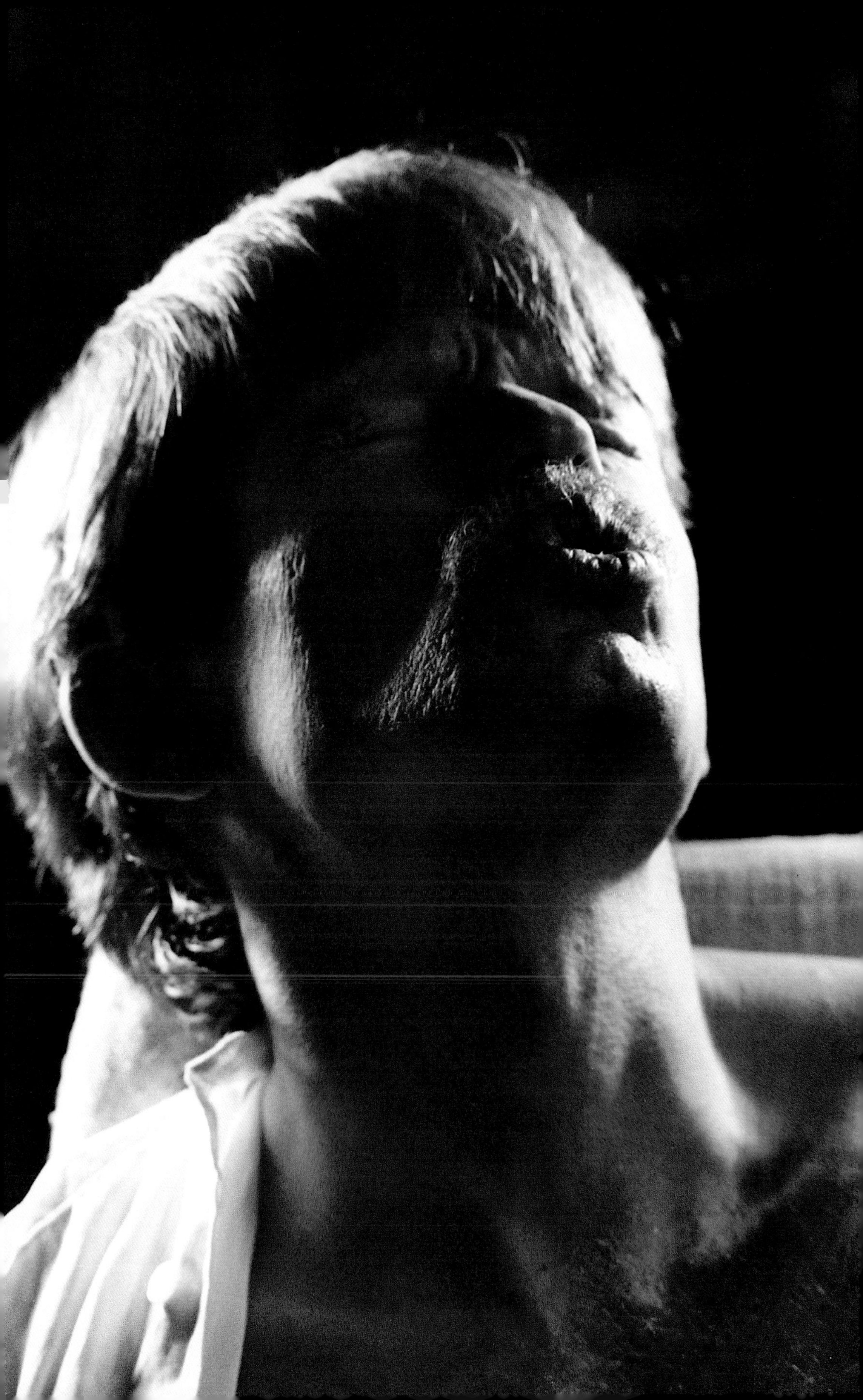

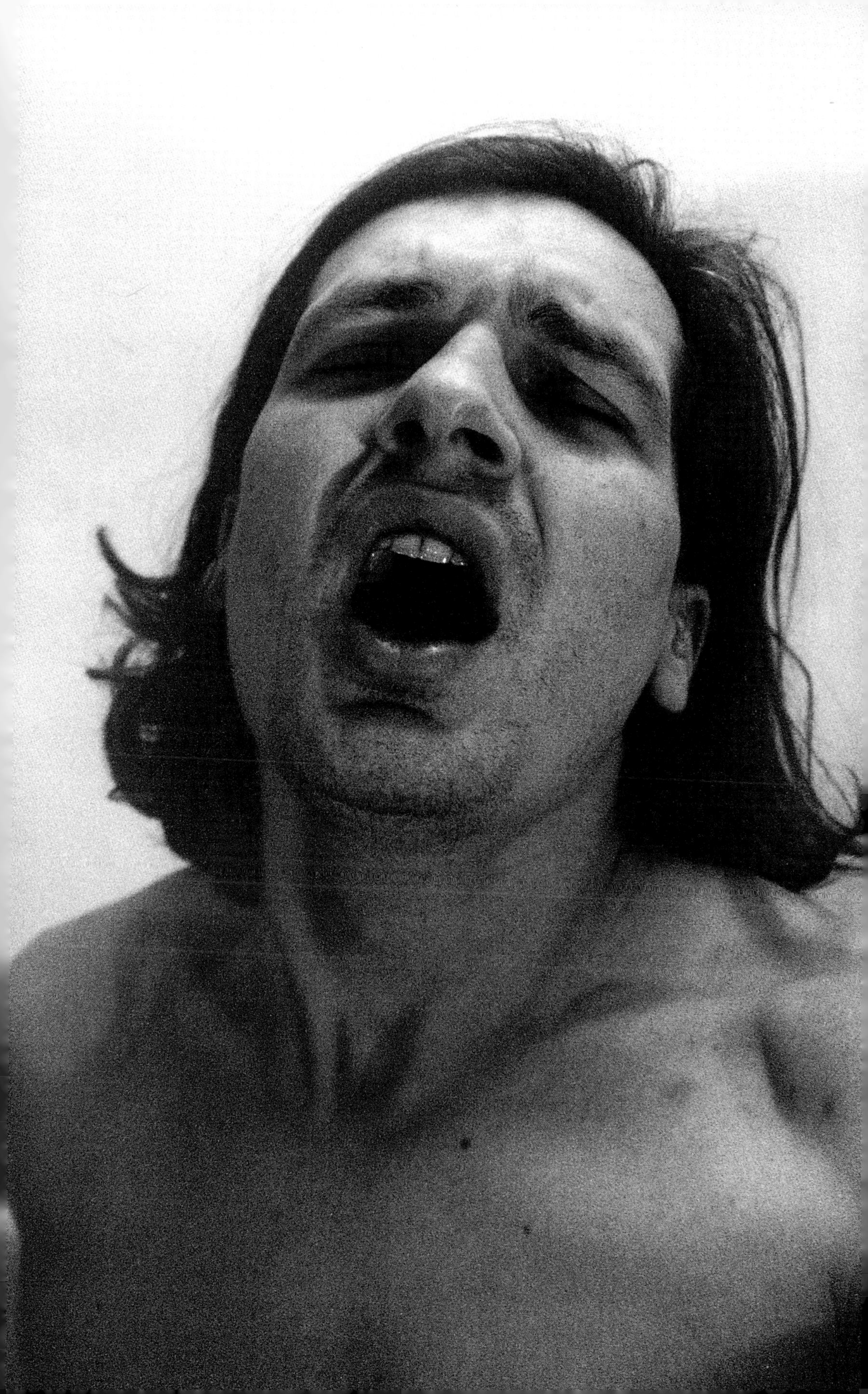

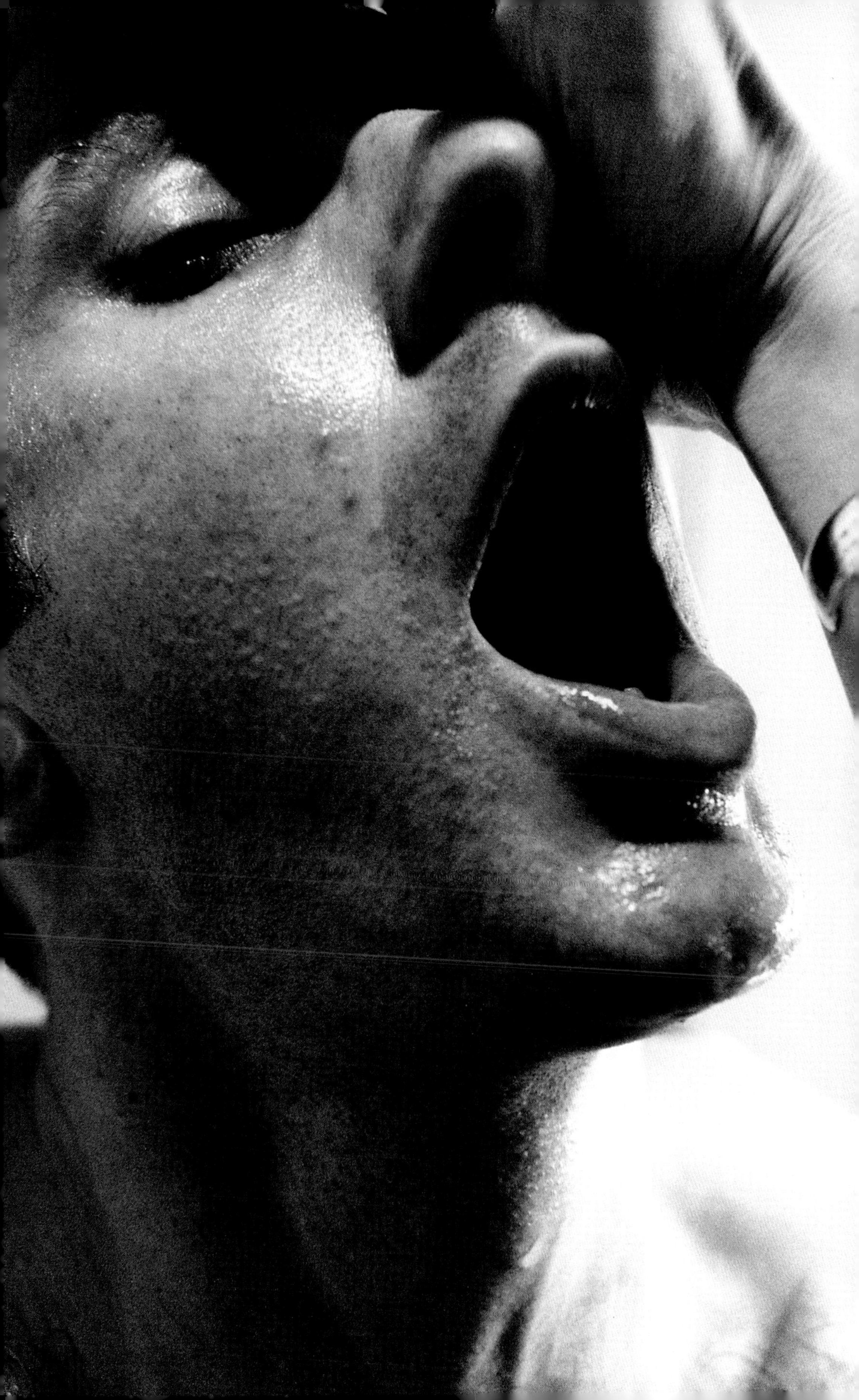

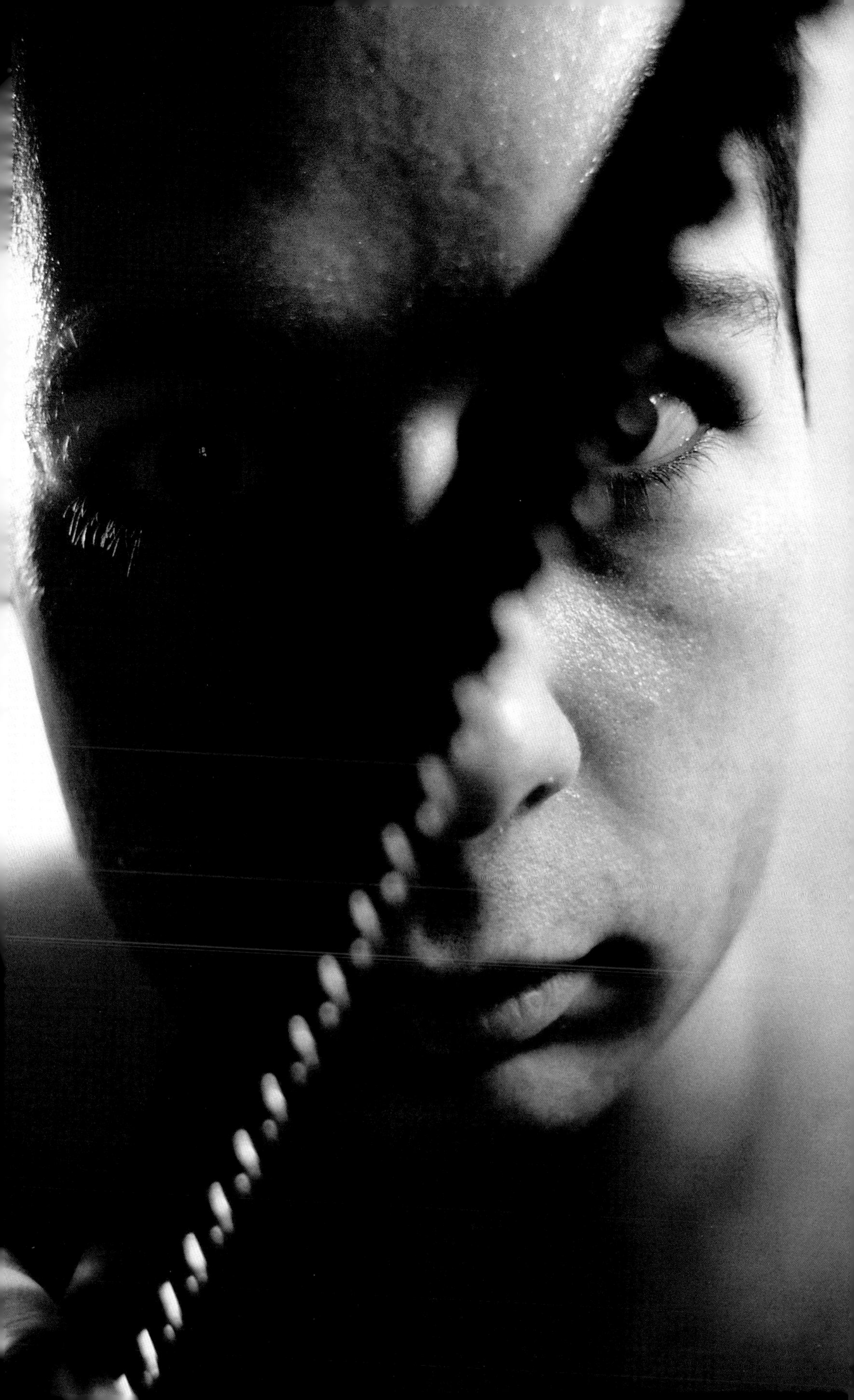

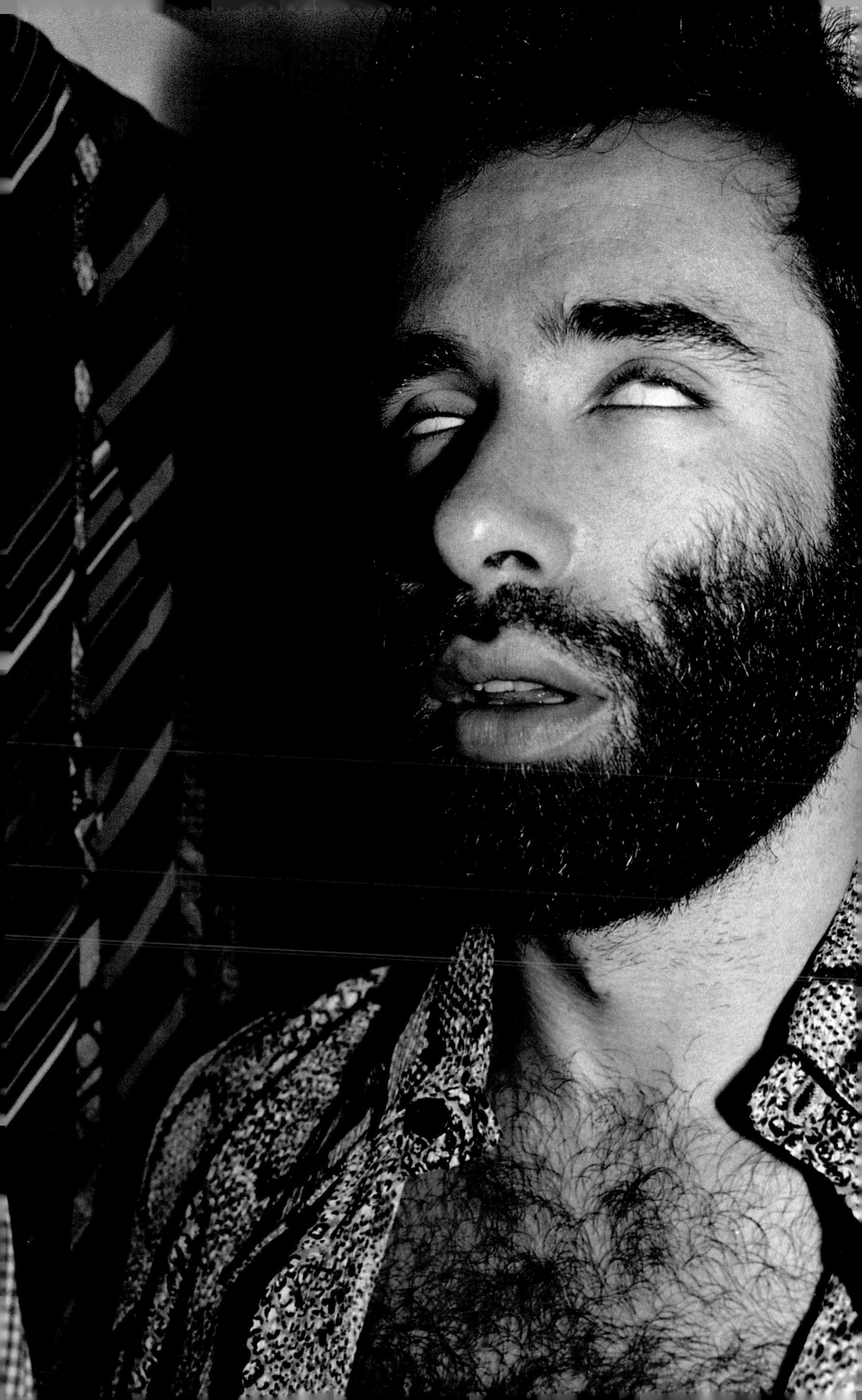

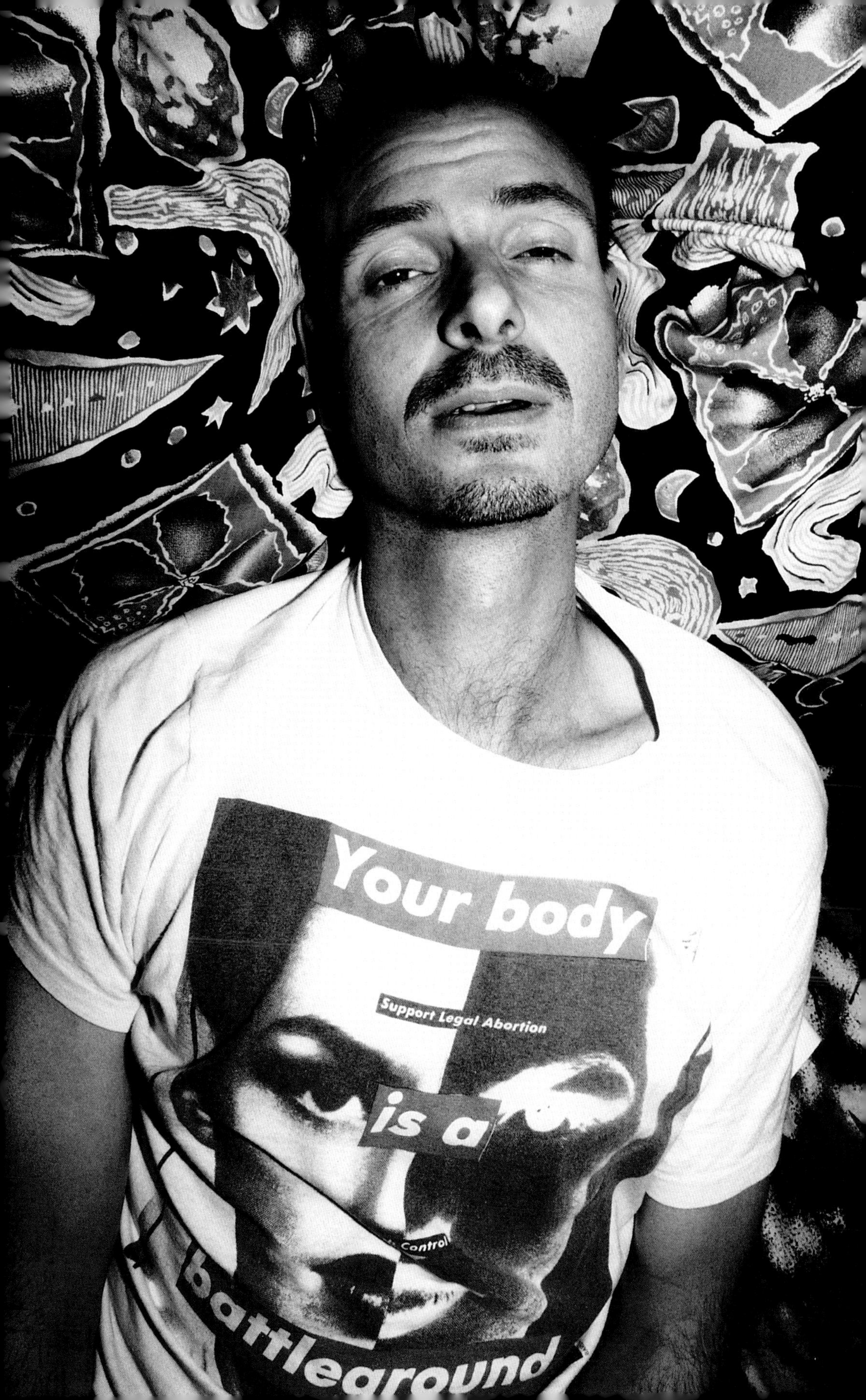

Your body
Support Legal Abortion
is a
Control
battleground

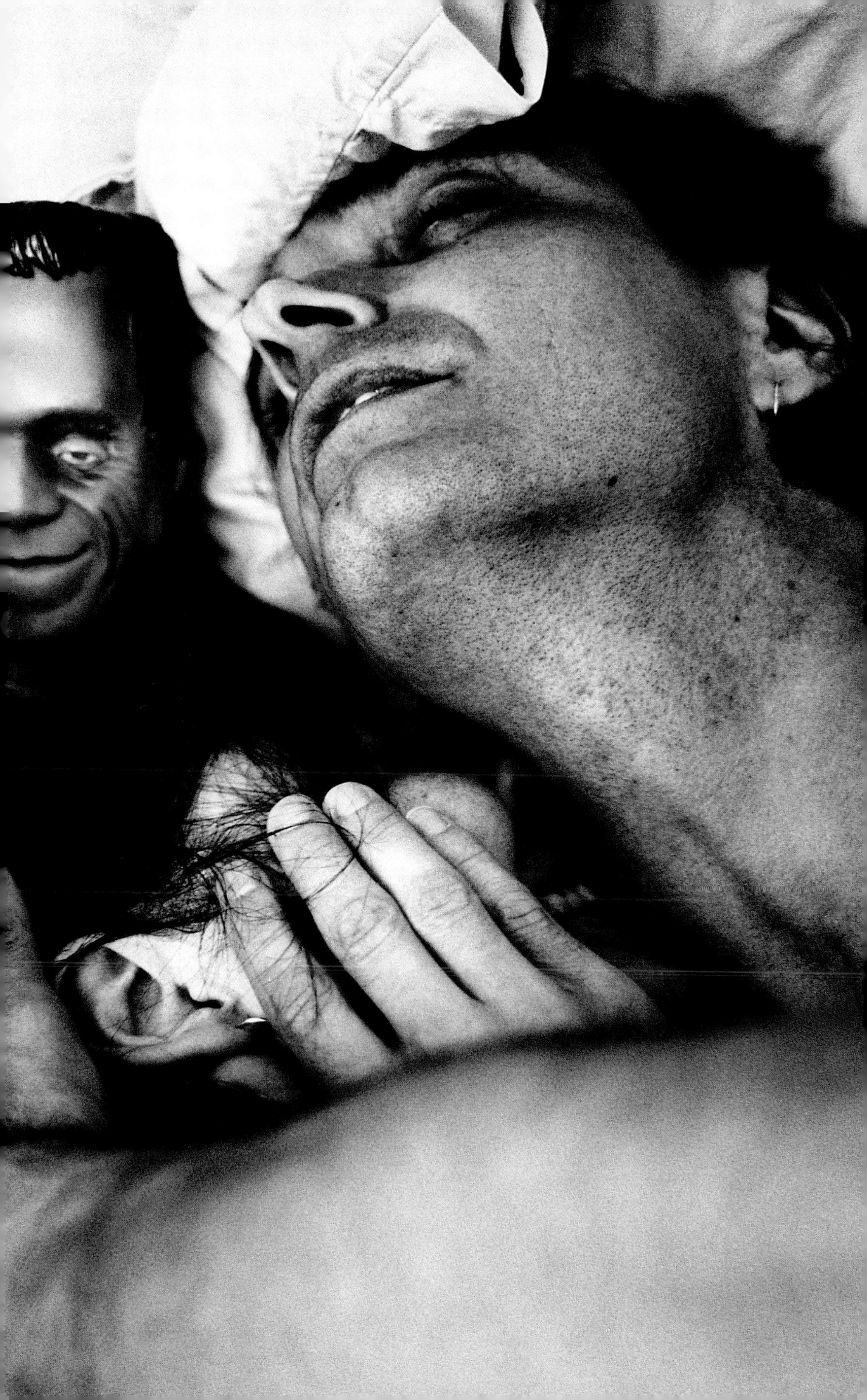

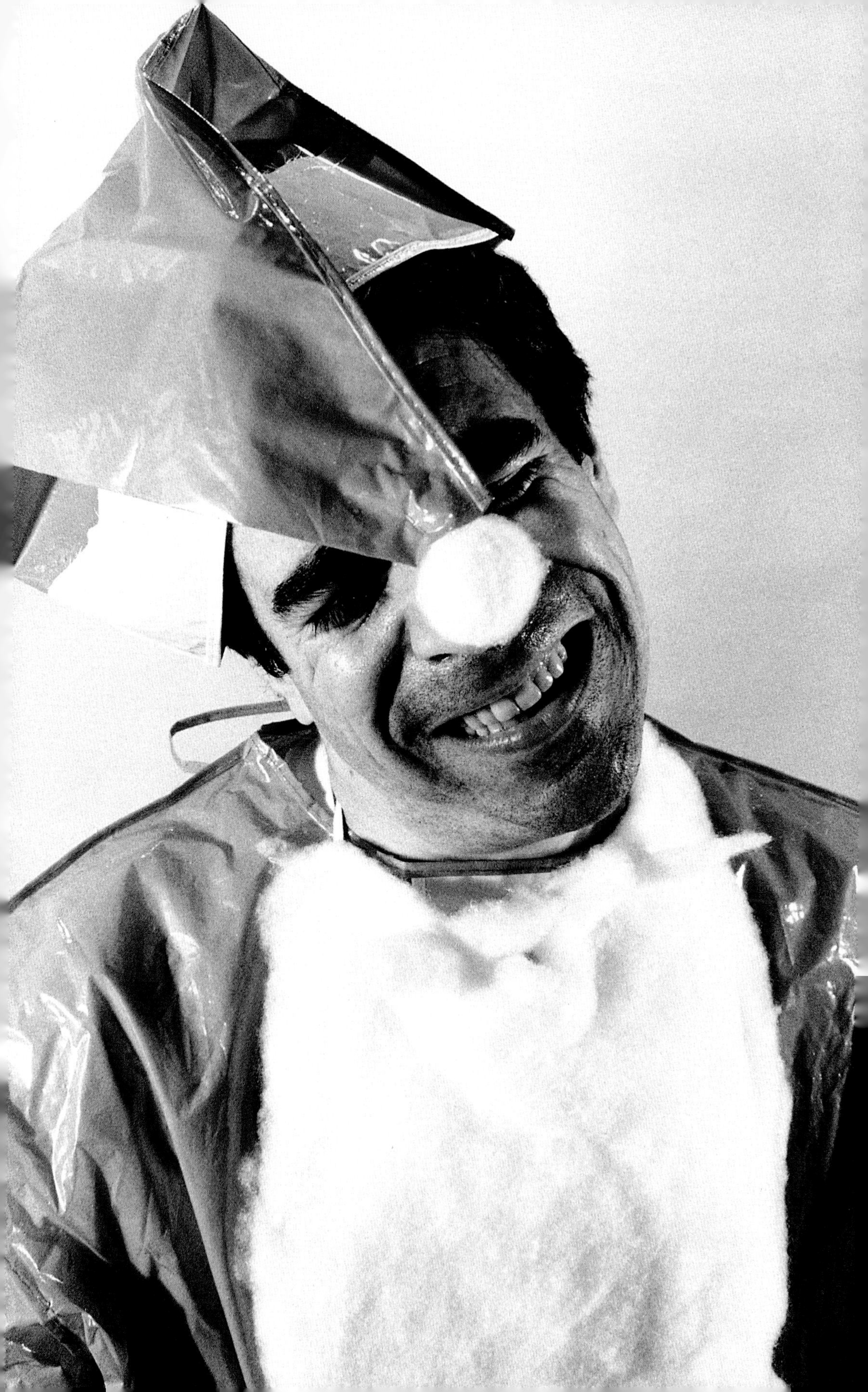

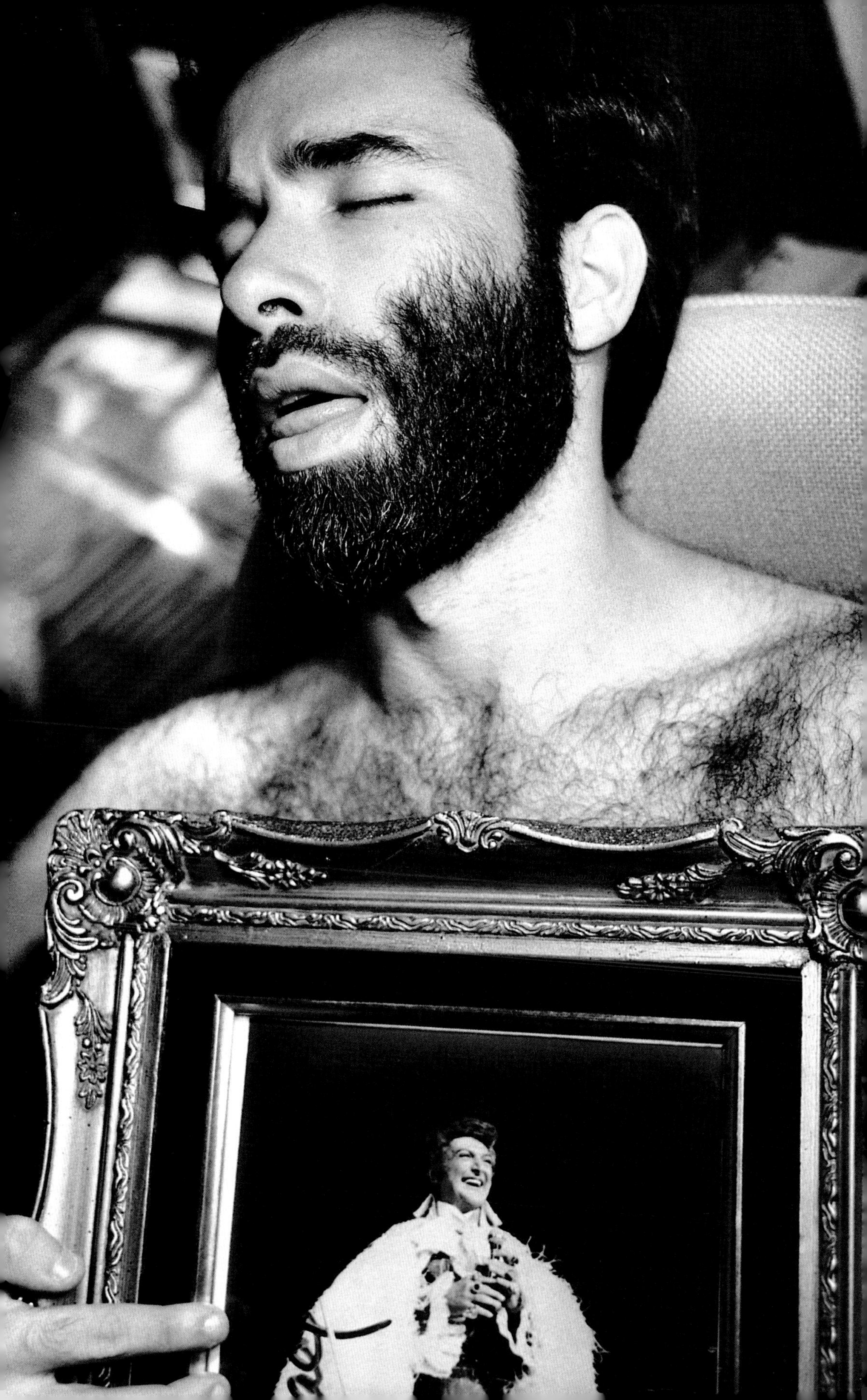

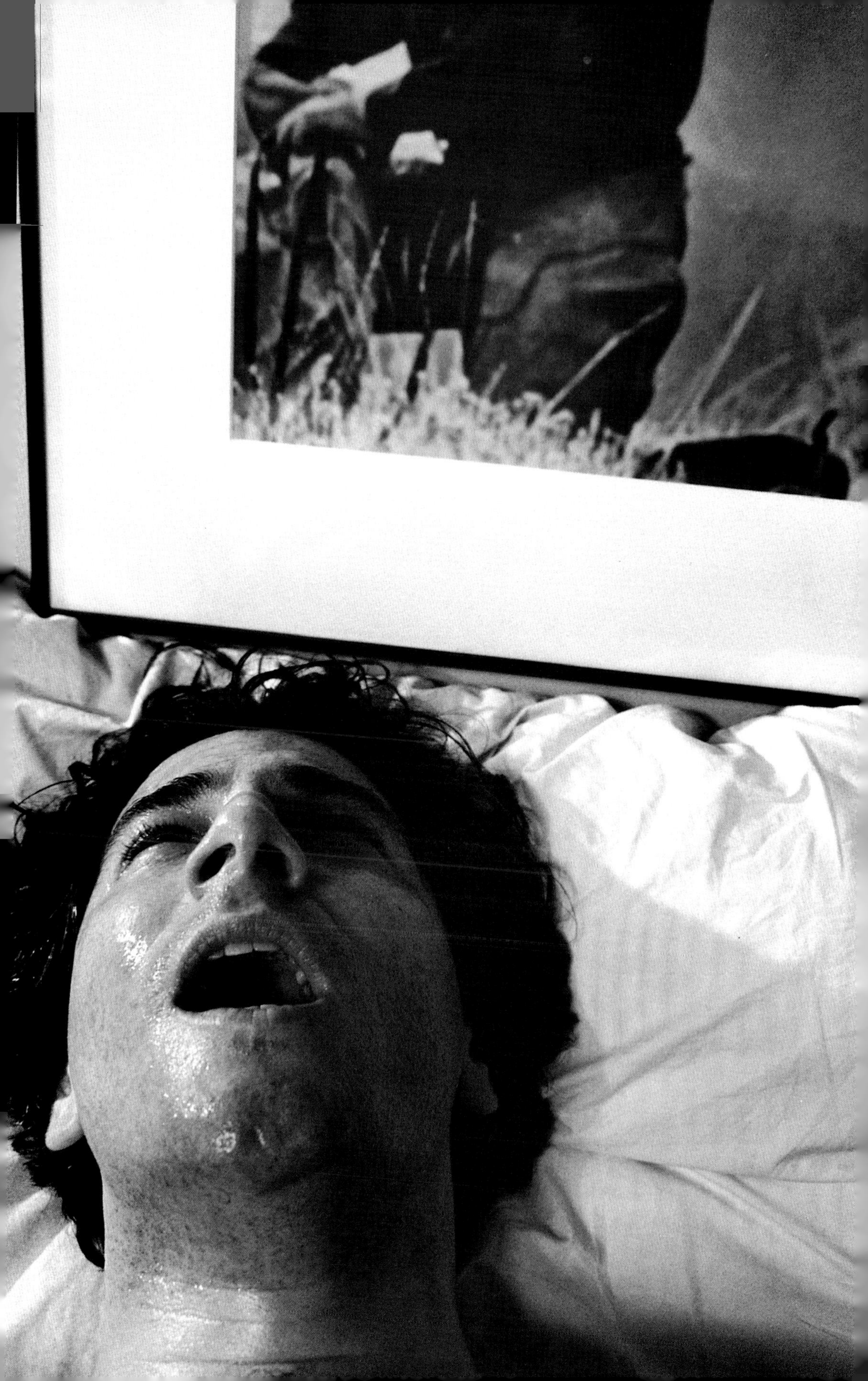

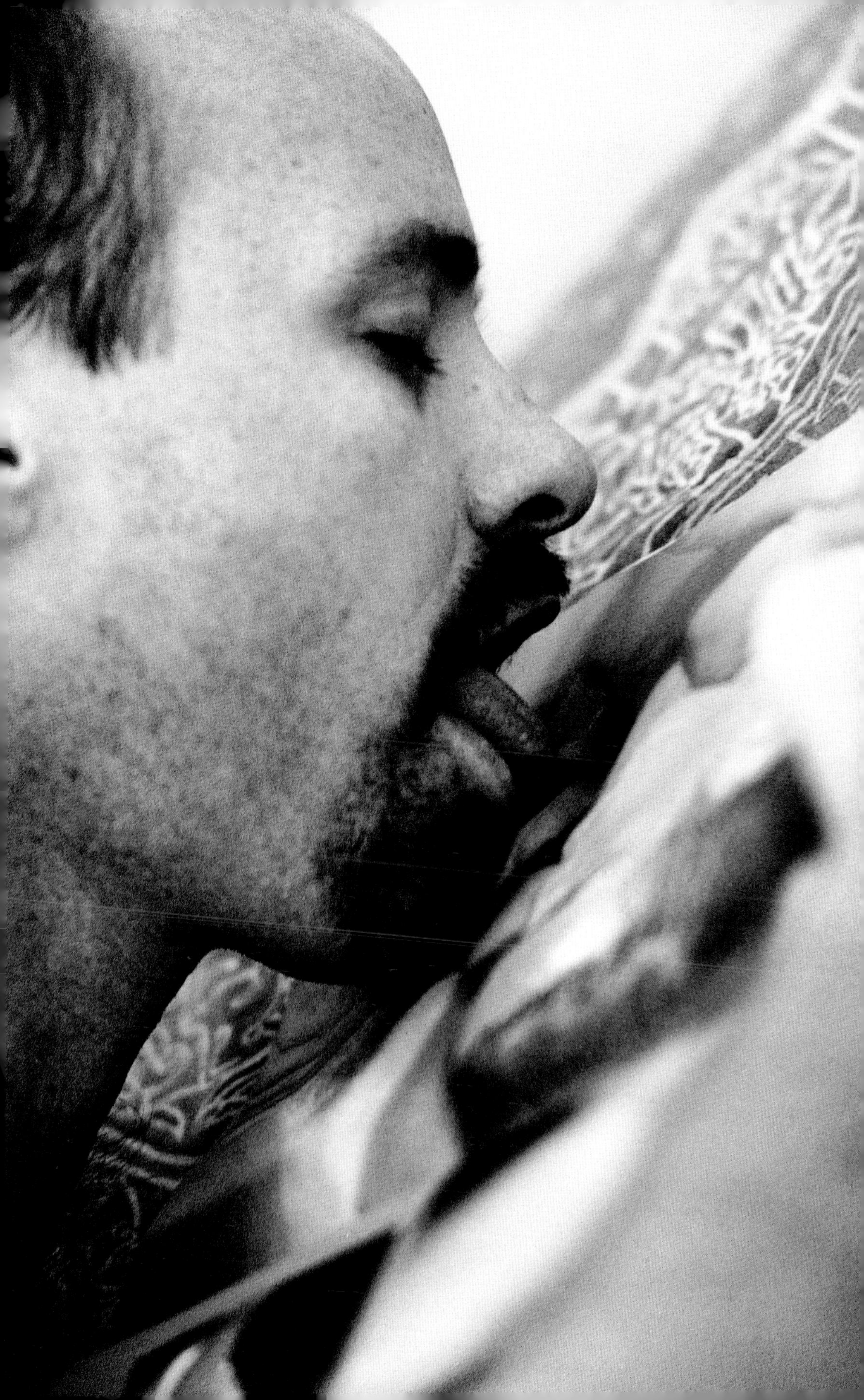

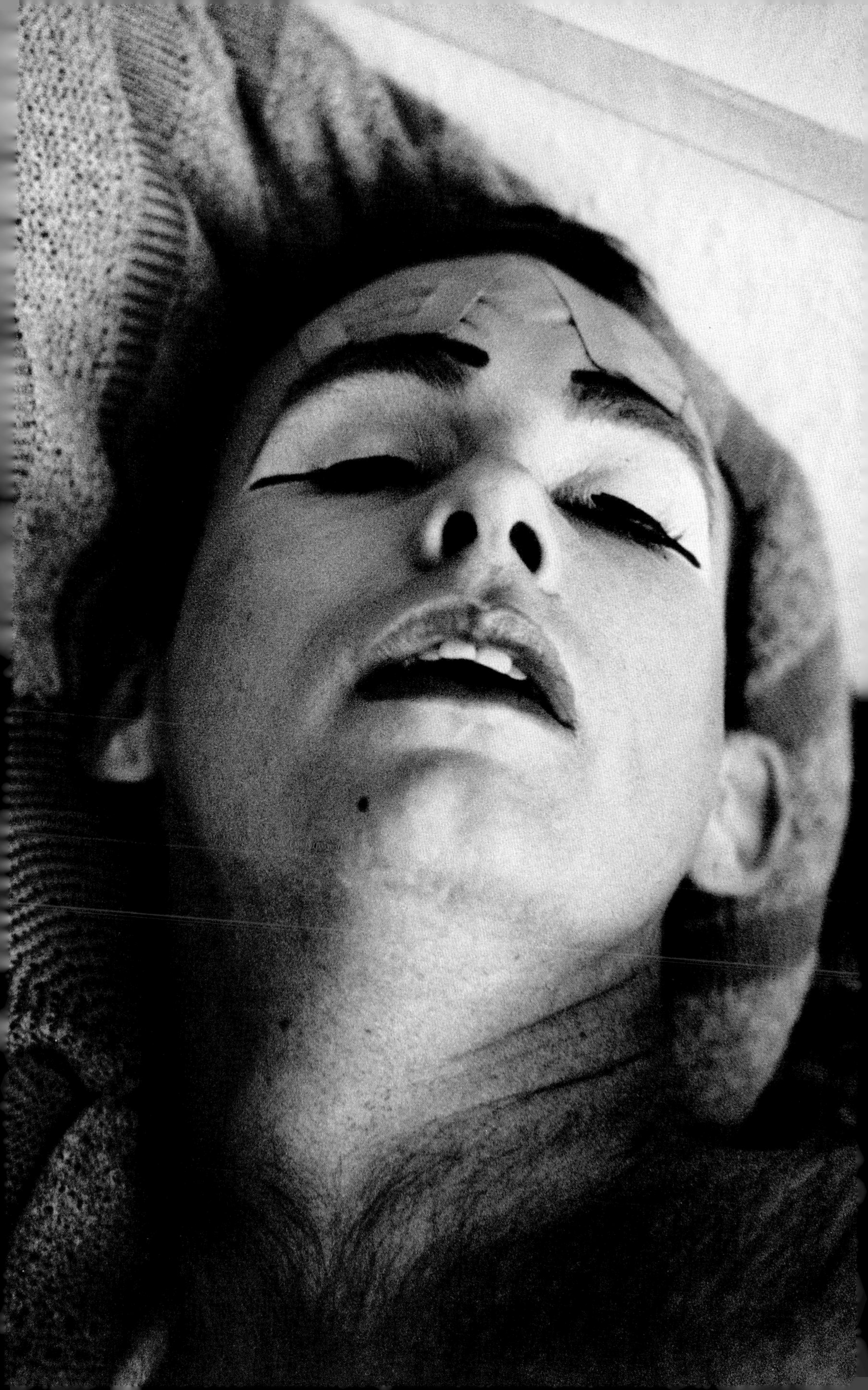

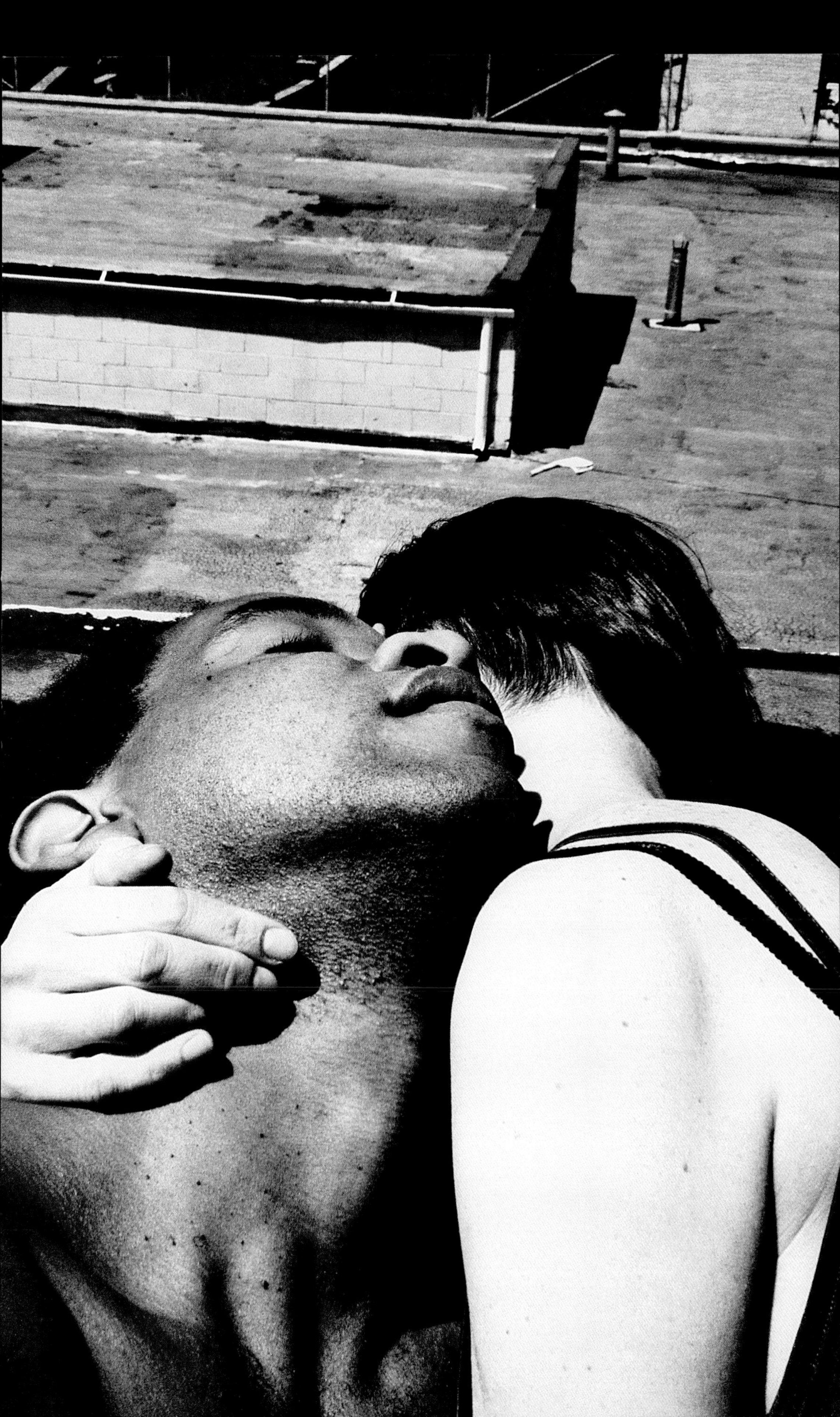

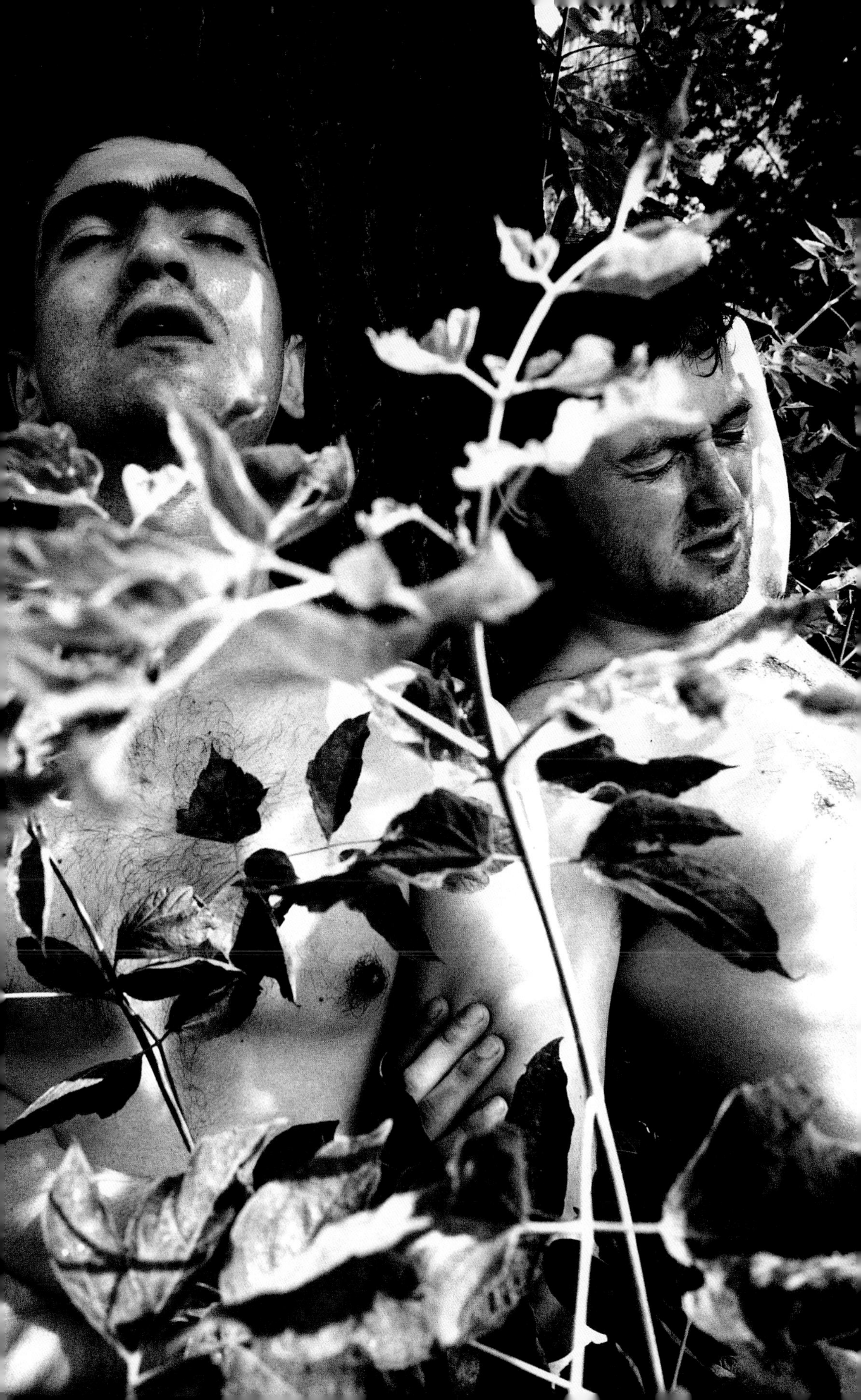

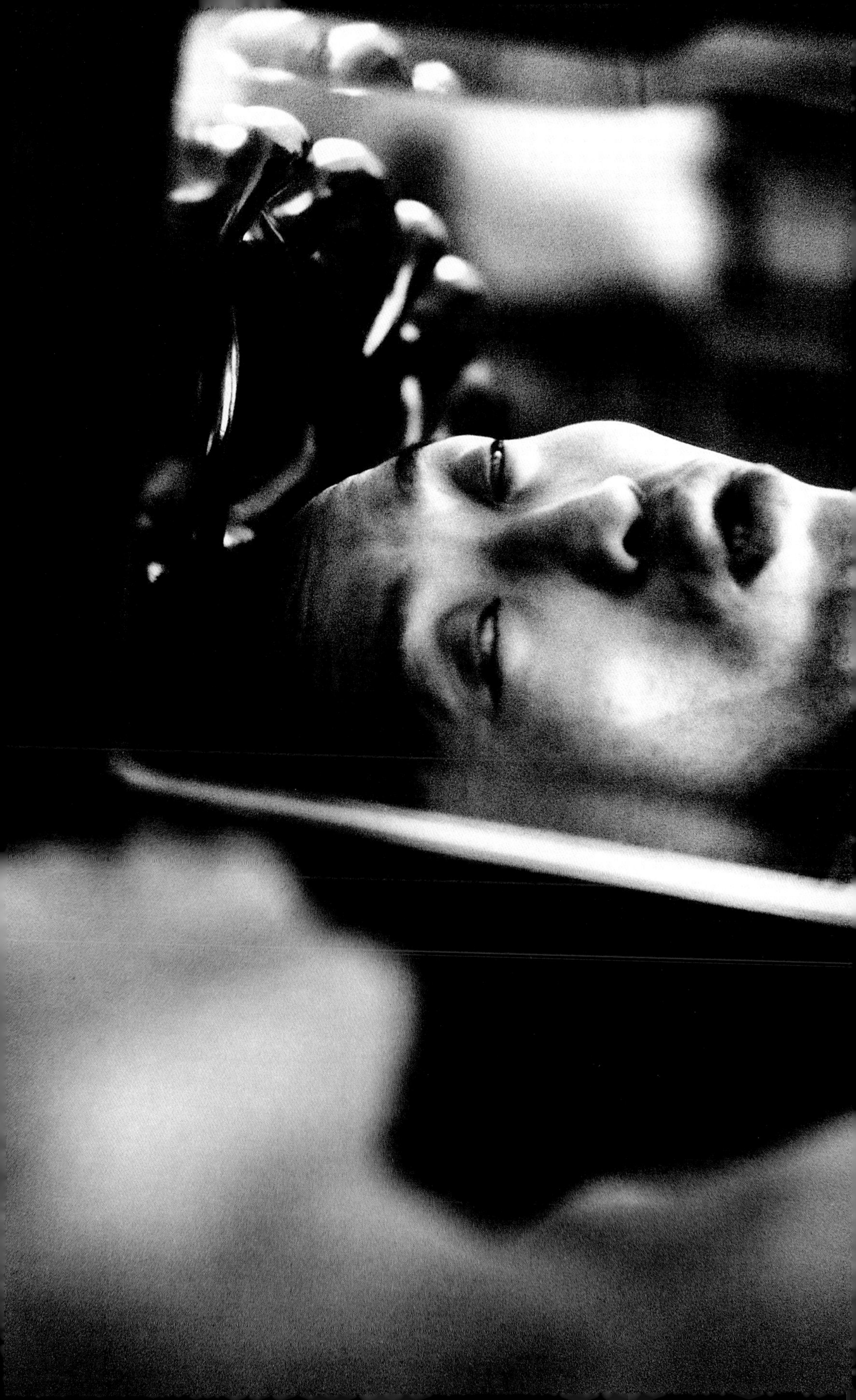